JANE AUSTEN'S
EMMA

SYDNEY STUDIES IN LITERATURE

FOUNDING EDITOR (1965-7): the late Professor K. G. W. Cross, then Head of the English Department, University of Newcastle

GENERAL EDITORS (1967-): G. A. Wilkes, Challis Professor of English Literature and Dr A. P. Riemer, Senior Lecturer in English Literature, University of Sydney

JANE AUSTEN'S

EMMA

J. F. BURROWS

Senior Lecturer in English
University of Sydney

SYDNEY UNIVERSITY PRESS

SYDNEY UNIVERSITY PRESS

Press Building, University of Sydney

NEW ZEALAND   Price Milburn and Company Limited
GREAT BRITAIN   Methuen and Company Limited, London
and their agents overseas

First published 1968

National Library of Australia registry number AUS 68-2072
Library of Congress Catalog Card Number 68-54902
SBN 424 05840 5

This book is supported by money from
THE ELEANOR SOPHIA WOOD BEQUEST

Printed in Australia at The Griffin Press, Adelaide
and registered in Australia for transmission by post as a book

CONTENTS

ACKNOWLEDGEMENTS

The author and publishers gratefully make acknowledgement to the following publishers for kind permission to include extracts from copyright works: Oxford University Press for *Emma* (The Oxford Illustrated *Jane Austen*) edited by Dr R. W. Chapman (3rd edn); Messrs Secker & Warburg for Professor Lionel Trilling's chapter '*Emma* and the Legend of Jane Austen' in his *Beyond Culture: Essays on Literature and Learning*; and Houghton Mifflin Company for Professor Trilling's Introduction to their edition of *Emma*.

PREFACE

Of the six novels on which Jane Austen's reputation chiefly rests, *Emma* (1816) was the last to be completed. Like *Mansfield Park* (1814), it was written entirely during her years at Chawton, the most settled period of her adult life. Both *Northanger Abbey* and *Persuasion* were published after her death in 1817. The former, which she had originally undertaken as early as 1797, was put aside a few months before she died; the latter, which she began after writing *Emma*, was never finished. With both *Sense and Sensibility* (1811) and *Pride and Prejudice* (1813), we know that the novel we have is more nearly as she wished it to be; but here, too, the effects of revision over many years are to be seen not only in puzzling shifts of tone but also in occasional loose ends. All four of these 'imperfect' novels exhibit Jane Austen's characteristic gifts and have given pleasure to innumerable readers. With none of them, however, can one proceed firmly on the assumption that even the tiniest detail is likely to form a meaningful part of the pattern.

In making that assumption and undertaking a minute examination of so well known and widely admired a novel as *Emma*, I have been influenced partly by the belief that some basic uncertainties of interpretation remain and, more powerfully, by the belief that *Emma* itself has riches yet in store. Although much valuable work has been done, critics of the English novel are only beginning to accept the implications of Henry James' conception of narrative art:

It is an incident for a woman to stand up with her hand resting on a table and look out at you in a certain way; or if it be not an incident I think it will be hard to say what it is. At the same time it is an expression of character. If you say you don't see it (character in *that—allons donc*!), this is exactly what the artist who has reasons of his own for thinking he *does* see it undertakes to show you.[1]

To approach *Emma* in the manner implied is to see certain of its qualities more clearly. Jane Austen raises serious issues and gives

---

1. Henry James, 'The Art of Fiction' (1884): in Leon Edel (ed.), *The House of Fiction*, London 1957, pp. 34-5.

7

them their just due. But those who isolate them from their proper context make her seem more earnest than she is. For hers is essentially a comic vision and she writes, as she has Emma speak, "with a sort of serious smile" (464).[2] Again, *Emma* shows a truly dramatic fluidity. If the novel is allowed to unfold naturally, one sees how sensitively its chief personages respond to each other and to the pressure of events. They are not static characters: when they deal in fixed ideas, they are soon taught better; and, as we shall see, the very words they use change meaning. To approach *Emma* as I have done is to discover, above all, how immeasurably a work of genius surpasses one's efforts to do it justice. One must hope, at best, that one's readers will be encouraged to return to the novel itself.

Without Dr Chapman's text, it would have been idle to attempt so detailed a study; and his associated writings have all been of great value. Of Jane Austen's many critics, I am indebted especially to Miss Lascelles, A. C. Bradley, Professor Trilling, Professor D. W. Harding, and Professor R. A. Brower.

It is a pleasure to acknowledge the many kindnesses shown me, in the course of my studies of Jane Austen, by Professor Geoffrey Tillotson, Dr Rosemary Freeman, Mr Duncan Isles, and Mr B. D. Greenslade; the editors of this series; Dr P. D. Edwards, Dr Jocelyn Harris, and Miss Margaret Harris; and by my wife, who bore the brunt. The responsibility for any imperfections in this study I naturally reserve to myself.

University of Sydney
June 1968

J. F. Burrows

---

2. All such unassigned references are to *Emma*, taken from Dr R. W. Chapman's edition. *See* Select Bibliography for other volumes of Dr Chapman's edition of Jane Austen's writings, referred to subsequently. Dr Chapman's edition of the novels restores their original division into volumes: in other modern editions of *Emma*, the chapters of Vol. ii are numbered 19-36, and those of Vol. iii, 37-55. Quotations from Jane Austen's works are shown within double quotation marks and all other interpolations within single.

INTRODUCTION

In *Emma*, as elsewhere, Jane Austen's art is in continual if unobtrusive motion. Hence it is not merely futile but positively misleading to rely on those fixed points of reference that can often simplify a critic's task. When the narrator's function varies subtly as occasion requires, the narrator cannot be regarded as consistently 'reliable' or, conversely, as consistently the voice of Emma's prejudices. When Mr Knightley is one fallible creature among others, he cannot be regarded as his author's spokesman and chief guardian of her values. When Emma's relationships with her fellows are incessantly in flux, she cannot be set against one character or beside another in large, stable contrasts and comparisons. When Emma's own moods vary with dazzling rapidity, it is idle to single out a passage for 'close reading' and to declare triumphantly that *this* is the real Emma. And when even the meaning supposedly enshrined in words like "reason", "imagination", "amiable", and "elegant" varies significantly as the novel proceeds, there can be no easy generalizing about Jane Austen's moral values. If these ideas hold good, it does not follow that *Emma* is without shape or meaning. It only follows that, instead of imposing an assumed meaning, a predetermined shape, upon the novel, we must let the novel work its effects on us.

Most of these matters can be left to evolve as our discussion proceeds. But certain problems associated with Mr Knightley must be faced at once. There is a moment late in the novel when, after reading John Knightley's reply to the news that his brother is to marry her, Emma remarks that:

"He writes like a sensible man. . . . I honour his sincerity. It is very plain that he considers the good fortune of the engagement as all on my side, but that he is not without hope of my growing, in time, as worthy of your affection, as you think me already. Had he said any thing to bear a different construction, I should not have believed him."

"My Emma, he means no such thing. He only means—"

"He and I should differ very little in our estimation of the two,"— interrupted she, with a sort of serious smile—"much less, perhaps, than

9

he is aware of, if we could enter without ceremony or reserve on the subject."

"Emma, my dear Emma—" (464)

Heedless of Mr Knightley's fond disclaimers and never pausing to remark Emma's capacity to speak so humbly and sincerely, those critics who most condemn the girl can join for once with her devotees. For she is offering, in effect, a paradigm of the novel as it is usually read. As it is usually read, *Emma* is concerned with its heroine's gradual progress to a point where she is no longer quite unworthy of the honour done her by Mr Knightley, spokesman for and apotheosis of Jane Austen's own values.

Few critics go so far as Professor Schorer who, in referring to 'the author (or, if you wish, Knightley)',[1] obliterates all distinction between the character and his creator. But more conservative opinion still makes no doubt of Mr Knightley's authority. Thus, for Professor Shannon, as representative as he is succinct, the novel is essentially concerned with 'Emma's progress from self-deception and vanity to perception and humility'; and 'the judicious Mr. Knightley, admired by all critics, is the yardstick against which Emma's conversion must be measured'.[2]

Like any literary yard-stick, this one gives different measurements in different hands. For most critics, Emma achieves true contrition. For a few devotees, perhaps, she has little to repent. And for a few determined ironists, her progress is illusory, her penitence transient, and her marriage doomed to fail. Thus the ultimate irony detected by Professor Mudrick is that 'there is no happy ending, no easy equilibrium, if we care to project confirmed exploiters like Emma and Churchill into the future of their marriages'.[3]

These differences as to the extent of Emma's progress are compounded by differences as to its exact nature. Is the long opposition between Mr Knightley and his protégée to be seen as an opposition between maturity and immaturity? Humility and arrogance? Altruism and self-concern? True freedom and petty licence? Reality and illusion? Reason and imagination? And yet, in all these variants, the area of discussion is really very limited: in all of them, Mr Knightley still sets the terms by which the opposition itself is to be defined and its resolution interpreted.

Mr Knightley's attitude to Frank Churchill gives rise, for some critics, to moments of doubt, which are customarily resolved in

1. Mark Schorer, 'The Humiliation of Emma Woodhouse' in Ian Watt (ed.), *Jane Austen*, p. 105.
2. Edgar F. Shannon, '*Emma*: Character and Construction', *PMLA*, Vol. lxxi (1956), pp. 650, 644.
3. Marvin Mudrick, *Jane Austen: Irony as Defense and Discovery*, p. 206.

comments on Jane Austen's awareness of human imperfection and which are not allowed to prejudice Mr Knightley's office as moral standard. So long as these and wider doubts are set aside, so long as Mr Knightley's obvious personal merits are used for raising him to the author's pedestal, so long as the reader believes himself possessed of an unfailing lodestone as he makes his way through the ironies of the novel—for so long as this, it is hard to accept that *Emma* fully deserves its reputation as a masterpiece. If Mr Knightley is his author's spokesman, Jane Austen's position is known to us, in all its essentials, by the end of the fifth chapter. In the four hundred pages that ensue before the predictable ending releases us at last, we are, it seems, to find what solace we can in the continuing infallibility— made so *human* by those little fallibilities—of Mr Knightley, in the charming but protracted follies of Emma, in the elaborate mystifica- tion about Frank Churchill, and in the satiric portrayal of sundry lesser worthies.

Only Professor Wright, I believe, has tried to grasp the nettle. In a statement whose implications he does not pursue, he suggests that it is time to re-open the whole question of Mr Knightley's authority:

Are we then to suppose that Emma is meant merely to exhibit the foibles of the world against a constant standard of values exemplified by Mr Knightley? Not at all: for then we should have seen him as the central figure, and the novel would have been a didactic treatise. Instead, Emma Woodhouse is the centre of attention and attraction.[4]

It is one thing to juggle terms like 'masterpiece' and to point to certain hypothetical advantages of questioning Mr Knightley's authority, quite another to show that it can in fact be questioned without distorting the text. Even in the passage with which we began, the passage where Emma comments on John Knightley's letter, there is at least one encouraging sign. In calling John Knightley "a sensible man", Emma repeats the phrase that marks his brother's first entry into the novel (9), a phrase that some critics have taken as an ultimate truth. The adjective is one that Jane Austen uses frequently, sometimes as pertaining to "sensibility" (as that fluid concept was understood in the eighteenth century), sometimes in the more modern sense dismissed in Johnson's *Dictionary*: '8. In low conversation it has sometimes the sense of reasonable; judicious; wise'. The older sense, I think, has no place here. In the 'low' modern sense, John Knightley may well be "sensible" to suppose that Emma is not yet worthy of the brother he so admires. But, notwithstanding Emma's magnanimity in using the

4. Andrew H. Wright, *Jane Austen's Novels: A Study in Structure*, pp. 159-60.

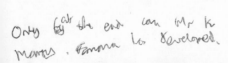
Only by the end can Mr K
merges. Emma is developed.

word of him, he carries frankness to the point of churlishness by being unremittingly "sensible" on such an occasion as this. It might be objected that this is carrying guilt by association to monstrous lengths, that Mr Knightley ought not to be condemned merely because an everyday phrase that is used of him—albeit in an emphatic context—is also used, four hundred pages later, of his too trenchant brother. But, whatever its exact meaning, "a sensible man" is not just an everyday phrase. In *Emma* itself, as we shall discover, it is used repeatedly, as are such variants as "men of sense"; and their increasing force culminates in an impressive dramatic irony (269). If Jane Austen's other novels are admitted as relevant comment, the matter grows more interesting still. It is no surprise to discover that the absurd Collins is not " 'a sensible man' " or that Mr Bennet has " 'great hopes of finding him quite the reverse' " (*Pride and Prejudice*, p. 64). But that ambiguous creature, Henry Crawford, is described by the narrator as "a man of sense" (*Mansfield Park*, p. 468). And even William Walter Elliot is admitted into the company. Suspicious as she is of his essential character, his cousin Anne is satisfied on this point:

Though they had now been acquainted a month, she could not be satisfied that she really knew his character. That he was a sensible man, an agreeable man,—that he talked well, professed good opinions, seemed to judge properly and as a man of principle,—this was all clear enough. He certainly knew what was right, nor could she fix on any one article of moral duty evidently transgressed; but yet she would have been afraid to answer for his conduct. She distrusted the past, if not the present. (*Persuasion*, p. 160)

My object is certainly not to suggest that Mr Knightley is another William Walter! It seems clear, however, that when he is first introduced as "a sensible man about seven or eight-and-thirty" (9), we ought not to leap to premature conclusions about his character, let alone his authority.

Nor is it true that Mr Knightley's jealousy of Frank Churchill is his only lapse from perfection. He himself is eventually to admit having misjudged Harriet Smith (331); to concede that, in spite of his earlier doubts, Emma has done Harriet good (474); and, above all, to acknowledge that his " 'interference' " with Emma " 'was quite as likely to do harm as good' " and, indeed, that " 'I do not believe I did you any good' " (462). All of these matters will require careful examination: but, lest his concessions be dismissed at once as blurred by his fondness for Emma, there is the fact that, when he and Emma are to marry, at least some of his neighbours think *he* has the better of the bargain (468).

As a final token that the question at issue may be worth reopening, there is a striking but neglected passage a little earlier in the novel, following immediately on Emma's acceptance of Mr Knightley's proposal of marriage, and uttered by the impersonal narrator: "This one half hour had given to each the same precious certainty of being beloved, had cleared from each the same degree of ignorance, jealousy, or distrust.—On his side, there had been a long-standing jealousy . . ." (432). Distracted perhaps by this last sentence, even those who have taken some account of Mr Knightley's jealousy can hardly have attended to the phrase, "the same degree of ignorance, jealousy, or distrust", or to the page of commentary that follows it. And yet that phrase, firmly if not patently supported by the commentary, puts the whole history of Emma and Mr Knightley in an uncommon light.

The question of Mr Knightley's authority, then, is easier to re-open than it may prove to close. But, before beginning the long and delicate task of exploring the novel without the usual lodestone, let us be clear about what is entailed. It is not a matter of writing a revolutionary 'character-sketch' of Mr Knightley, somehow finding —or inventing—grounds for declaring him a knave, fool, or prig. It is a matter of accepting him as a leading but not oracular partici-pant in the interplay of speech and action that makes up the novel, a matter of heeding his words but not bowing to them. When he is regarded in this way, one is freed from his dominance and enabled to look not merely at him but at the whole novel in an altered light. In that light, as I hope I am capable of showing, *Emma* appears more subtly amusing, more richly meaningful, and more thoroughly dramatic.

CHAPTER I
Volume One

I

Emma Woodhouse, handsome, clever, and rich, with a comfortable home and happy disposition, seemed to unite some of the best blessings of existence; and had lived nearly twenty-one years in the world with very little to distress or vex her.

Even familiarity does not dull these opening ironies. Behind the sunny aspect of Miss Woodhouse's fortunate situation in life lies a premonitory antithesis between those of "the best blessings of existence" that she "seemed to unite" and those "real evils" (5) whose danger "was at present so unperceived, that they did not by any means rank as misfortunes with her" (5-6). The "seemed", "unperceived", and "with her" mark a narrative mode as unobtrusive as it is exact. Where certainty is called for, we are allowed to be certain: the second and third paragraphs touch on a whole history of indulgence, leaving no doubt why "the power of having rather too much her own way, and a disposition to think a little too well of herself" (5) have come to be the real evils of Emma's situation. Yet, where Emma's future comes into account, the narrator speaks less plainly. If she is possessed of only some of the best blessings of existence, what others are lacking? The opening catalogue fails to reckon any conspicuously moral attributes. But, though their absence stirs the attention, it serves chiefly to keep a crucial issue open. Again, the time is to come when Emma herself will see the best of blessings as lying in the love and companionship of marriage: ". . . if Harriet were to be the chosen, the first, the dearest, the friend, the wife to whom he looked for all the best blessings of existence" (422-3). But neither Emma nor the reader can know this when the novel begins: here, too, the narrator falls silent. To the modern reader, "happy disposition" seems plain enough: but we should recall that "disposition" once bore a less passive sense. The distinction between 'temper of mind' and 'tendency to any act or state' (as Johnson has it) hardly needs the support of a dictionary. Yet Johnson illustrates the latter sense with

15

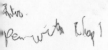

Intro.
Pen with Chap 1

a highly pertinent passage from Locke: '*Disposition* is when the power and ability of doing any thing is forward, and ready upon every occasion to break into action.' Since Jane Austen uses the word in both senses (e.g. 58, 18) we cannot know what was in her mind. We are soon to discover, however, that Emma is less gifted with contentment itself than with a readiness 'upon every occasion to break into action' in its pursuit; and we may suppose that her "happy disposition" is two-edged. If, finally, there is nothing ambiguous about Emma's having almost attained the great age of twenty-one, there are delicate ironic reverberations around the phrase signalizing her achievement: "nearly twenty-one years in the world". Sheltered all her life in Highbury, she can scarcely be said to have lived in the world at all.

The world that Emma does know is in no small measure a world of book-fed imaginings. Even though their relationship is concealed by Jane Austen's ever-growing unobtrusiveness, Emma is cousin-german to Catherine Morland and kinswoman to other fanciful young heroines. One thinks especially of the female Quixotes,[1] their experience inflated and their understanding distorted by an over-heated fancy. Thus, when Emma first appears, reflecting on Miss Taylor's marriage, her fancy speaks at once. That she should regret the loss of such a companion is obviously not fanciful; and her later excesses are as nothing beside the extravagance of her father's lamentations for "poor Miss Taylor" (8, *et passim*). All such qualifications notwithstanding, Emma's mood grows more and more bookish as she sits that evening, another Emily de St Aubert, "in mournful thought of any continuance" and admitting no occupation but to "think of what she had lost" (6). Long afterwards, on a truly sorrowful occasion, Emma herself is to look back wryly on this mood of "melancholy fancy" (422).

Not that she has long to cultivate it. Her father's waking obliges her to attend to his plaintive 'ands' and querulous 'buts' and to take up the cheerful, simple-spoken, and patiently repetitive tones that mark her whole intercourse with him. The narrator may well comment that, while "he could not meet her in conversation, rational or playful" (7), Emma, for her part, "spared no exertions" (9). If we cannot regard Mr Woodhouse as affectionately as she

---

1. As her *Letters* (p. 173) show, Jane Austen thought highly of Charlotte Lennox's amusing novel, *The Female Quixote; or, The Adventures of Arabella* (1752). But the evidence generally favours the suggestion that, though "*Emma* . . . presents a deliberately contrived antithesis between the worlds of actuality and illusion . . . I think Jane Austen had no particular novel or comedy of intrigue in mind" (Mary Lascelles, *Jane Austen and Her Art*, pp. 68-9). As we shall see, Emma's language is bookish rather than directly allusive.

does, it is chiefly because we are made aware of what he is doing to her. Towards his neighbours, it is true, he is kindly, courteous, and as generous as his understanding permits. Even when he imposes his terrors of wedding-cake, sea-bathing, or asparagus on physiques less delicate than his own, his goodwill at least cannot be questioned. And, in graver matters like the Bates' poverty, he shows a real benevolence and another kind of delicacy. Towards Emma, however, his affectionate intentions are smothered by his endless trivial demands. Worse still, he and the mediocrities whom he summons to Hartfield make feeble company for so lively and intelligent a being. And, worst of all, they join with him in lauding her every action. Small wonder that Emma waxes self-important; that her life in Highbury leaves her more discontented than she knows; and that, scarcely consciously, she bedecks her dull surroundings in the trappings of romance.

Emma's exertions on her father's behalf are relieved, for that evening at least, by a neighbourly visit from Mr Knightley, whose manner of addressing Mr Woodhouse contrasts delightfully with hers. Not for him those never-wearying efforts to enlighten a mind that admits no ray. With Mr Woodhouse, as with almost everyone, Mr Knightley is courteously laconic. He states his conviction, supplies his evidence, and has done: " 'Not at all, sir. It is a beautiful, moonlight night; and so mild that I must draw back from your great fire' " (10); " 'Dirty, sir! Look at my shoes. Not a speck on them' " (10).

Even in this first chapter, however, the voice of downright commonsense proves less apt on a more delicate subject. Emma's earlier broodings have shown that her emotions about the marriage are various but intense. There is a keen sense of personal loss. There is a generous sense of Miss Taylor's advantage, both emotional and material, in marrying "a man of unexceptionable character, easy fortune, suitable age and pleasant manners" (6). And, in a minor but utterly characteristic key, there is a sense of personal satisfaction in having "always wished and promoted the match" (6). Yet, in seeking to assuage Emma's regret, Mr Knightley can suggest only that, by material standards, Miss Taylor has made a good match. In his little sermon on advantageous marriage—its purpose crudely veiled by its being ostensibly addressed to Mr Woodhouse, its omissions laid bare by the paternalistic "she knows how much" and "she knows how very acceptable"—the culminating "happily" is almost obtusely prosaic:

"It is impossible that Emma should not miss such a companion," said Mr. Knightley. "We should not like her so well as we do, sir, if we could suppose it. But she knows how much the marriage is to Miss Taylor's advantage; she knows how very acceptable it must be at Miss Taylor's time of life to be settled in a home of her own, and how important to her to be secure of a comfortable provision, and therefore cannot allow herself to feel so much pain as pleasure. Every friend of Miss Taylor must be glad to have her so happily married."(11)

Stung by his evident belief that she needs such reminders, Emma replies in a way that sets off the first of those disputes which do so much to define the course of the novel, which display the characteristic powers and limitations of both participants, and which reveal the deep misunderstandings that divide them. For, concealing the fact that she is "divided between tears and smiles" (11), Emma adopts the air of a latter-day Millamant, insisting that she made the match and that " 'to have it take place, and be proved in the right . . . may comfort me for any thing' " (12). Only encouraged in this brittle gaiety by Mr Knightley's admonitory shake of the head and her father's mournful admiration for her genius, she rushes on into ever more fanciful embroiderings of the small original fact that, against her own selfish interests, "she had always wished and promoted the match" (6).

It is too much for Mr Knightley. Either she has been so indelicate as actively to promote the match or she is being so frivolous as to congratulate herself on a lucky guess. Besides separating the two possibilities that he sees into strict alternatives, he states each of them in a harsher form than the facts warrant: in his account it is a matter of either " 'endeavouring for the last four years' " or " 'saying to yourself one idle day' " (12).

For a moment Emma grows sarcastic but then, her whole tone changing, she makes him a serious and not unconciliatory reply:

"You have drawn two pretty pictures—but I think there may be a third— a something between the do-nothing and the do-all. If I had not promoted Mr. Weston's visits here, and given many little encouragements, and smoothed many little matters, it might not have come to any thing after all. I think you must know Hartfield enough to comprehend that." (13)

Given Mr Woodhouse's fussiness in general and his dislike for marriage in particular, Emma must surely have needed to smooth "many little matters"; and, given Mr Knightley's standing as "a very old and intimate friend of the family" (9), he "must know Hartfield enough to comprehend that".

By now, however, Mr Knightley is in no mood to refine his original distinction. Ignoring both the weight of her defence and her change of tone, he can talk only of the ability of sensible people to manage their own affairs and of Emma's needless " 'interference' " (13). More conscious of an advantage to others than of his own

18

interference, he is long afterwards to smooth the way to a marriage that he has himself wished and promoted: he sends Robert Martin on business to his brother's house when Harriet Smith is a guest there. But this, I think, is less a satiric shaft than a reminder that, by then, he has achieved the gentler wisdom that enables him to admit his own " 'interference' " (462) with Emma.

In the meantime, this is no way to address Miss Woodhouse. No longer hoping to placate him, she returns to the attack. With the merest pretence of addressing her father, who has been trudging along in the wake of the argument and "understanding but in part" (13), she declares that she has another protégé in mind: " 'Only one more, papa; only for Mr. Elton. Poor Mr. Elton! You like Mr. Elton, papa,—I must look about for a wife for him' " (13). Mr Knightley has the last word; but, though he can predict how Elton will behave, he cannot treat Emma tactfully. With ill-timed glee, he snatches at a hint from Mr Woodhouse and relegates Emma to the housekeeping: " 'Invite him to dinner, Emma, and help him to the best of the fish and the chicken, but leave him to chuse his own wife. Depend upon it, a man of six or seven-and-twenty can take care of himself' " (14).

When Emma's talk of match-making and Mr Knightley's forecast about Elton are considered in their context, Emma's behaviour assumes a more favourable aspect, Mr Knightley's a less, than when these celebrated instances are seen in isolation. Yet it is not enough simply to invert received opinion. Emma's true feelings about Miss Taylor's marriage are obscured by her attempt to appear worldly. Yet, in the months that follow, her giving of little encouragements and smoothing of little matters is to harden into precisely such interference as is now laid unjustly at her door. Mr Knightley's part in this first dispute does not, one would have thought, conduce to that complete faith in his judgement that leads to his being identified with the author. Yet one's sense of his shortcomings is tempered by the reflection that he does not share our access to Emma's mind but must address himself to what she says and does. He is perhaps as bewildered by the freaks of her fancy as she is irritated by his reduction of complex emotions to tangible simplicities.

Mr Knightley's little joke about choosing a good dinner for Mr Elton marks the end of the first chapter, an opportune moment to take up certain questions of narrative method. Theorists of the novel have sometimes assumed that impersonal narration and the so-called 'point-of-view' technique differ so radically that a whole novel will—or even should—be cast in one only of these modes. Mere practising critics, however, have long recognized that, in *Emma* for example, the third-person narrator speaks at times impersonally, at other times for Emma herself, for Mr Knightley, and, even now and again, for non-characters like the Campbells (164) and Perry the apothecary (389). In reading such a novel, we can only rely on the writer to show us what authority to vest in one passage or another. For, when the narrator speaks from the point of view of a particular character, we know only that such and such is that character's belief: but, when the narrator speaks impersonally, we can simply accept what we are told.

Even the most rewarding of recent theorists, Professor Wayne Booth, does not always respond to the tiny but accurate cues by which Jane Austen guides us. In the following comment, I submit, each of the examples given raises doubts where there need be none:

> Whenever we leave the "real evils" we have been warned against in Emma, the narrator's and Emma's views coincide: we cannot tell which of them, for example, offers the judgment on Mr. Woodhouse that "his talents could not have recommended him at any time," or the judgment on Mr. Knightley that he is "a sensible man," "always welcome" at Hartfield, or even that "Mr. Knightley, in fact, was one of the few people who could see faults in Emma Woodhouse, and the only one who ever told her of them."[2]

The tiny cues I speak of, ranging from virtual stage directions to delicate shifts of tone or address, can be seen, to begin with, in two early accounts of Mr Weston:

> The event had every promise of happiness for her friend. Mr. Weston was a man of unexceptionable character, easy fortune, suitable age and pleasant manners; and there was some satisfaction in considering ... (6);

> Mr. Weston was a native of Highbury, and born of a respectable family, which for the last two or three generations had been rising into gentility and property. He had received a good education, but on succeeding early in life to a small independence... (15).

Everything here lies within the presumable scope of Emma's knowledge but, whereas the facts of the former passage are intimately related to Emma's hopes for Miss Taylor, those of the latter are comparatively remote from Emma's concerns. Emma's implied presence in the former passage is more definitely marked by such cues as "her friend", her "satisfaction in considering", and even "unexceptionable", the word of a person alert for grounds on which to take exception. In the latter passage, however, there are no such personal touches. Each passage, finally, is appropriate to its context: the former is part of Emma's private reflections in the first chapter while the latter is the impersonal narrator's opening of the second.

Returning, then, to Professor Booth's examples, I submit that the

2. Wayne C. Booth, *The Rhetoric of Fiction*, p. 257.

first issues a harsher and more epigrammatic judgement of Mr Woodhouse than Emma would entertain; that it reaches back into a period of his life beyond Emma's cognizance; and that it falls within a paragraph separated on no other ground from her preceding and succeeding reflections. Of the judgements of Mr Knightley, the first two phrases could conceivably come from Emma herself. But the one is too cool, the other too self-evident, to come naturally from Emma's mind; and both fall within a paragraph of detached exposition where, for example, John Knightley is referred to not as "her brother" but as "Isabella's husband". The last and most significant judgement cannot be Emma's at all: she can hardly know of those who see faults in her without saying so; and the "in fact" and the "Emma Woodhouse" mark the sentence off as the impersonal narrator's comment on what the characters are saying. As the novel proceeds and Jane Austen increasingly assumes our familiarity with her methods, there are cases more subtle than these: the more reason, then, not to create difficulties where none exist.

II

Jane Austen now begins to look a little further afield. In the second and third chapters a more conventional narrator briskly recounts the events leading to the Westons' marriage and then turns to other members of the little circle surrounding Hartfield. In the development of *Emma*, these more straightforward chapters play a necessary part. The relationship between Emma and Mr Knightley could not subsist in a vacuum; yet Emma is not the witness one would choose to supply one's first knowledge of her fellows. Again, the narrator's manner is admirably suited to the introduction of matters which we need to know but which, for the time being, we must not be encouraged to consider deeply:

> Mr. Frank Churchill was one of the boasts of Highbury, and a lively curiosity to see him prevailed, though the compliment was so little returned that he had never been there in his life. His coming to visit his father had been often talked of but never achieved. (17)

These more straightforward chapters are by no means dull. A few crisp sentences dispose of the interminable tea-parties where, with all the gravity of Parliament, "it was very generally proposed", without "a dissentient voice", that Frank Churchill must now come and where everyone assembled finds in "handsome", repeated four times in a few lines, the only epithet worthy of his recent letter to his father (17-18). Three months later, that letter and that epithet still supply Mr Woodhouse with conversation (96). For Mrs Weston, however, the letter is "highly-prized" (18): in a single word she is distinguished from the chorus.

Emma, meanwhile, has accepted the loss of Miss Taylor and now finds a warm satisfaction in Mrs Weston's happiness. Emma's own needs, however, have not been supplied. Despite her pleasure for her father's sake, she has little to hope from "the quiet prosings of three such women" (22) as the Bateses and Mrs Goddard. But Mrs Goddard soon afterwards requests, "in most respectful terms, to be allowed to bring Miss Smith with her" that evening; and Emma, in the role of "fair mistress of the mansion", returns " a very gracious invitation" (22). Let us defer Miss Smith's entrance a little longer: while her association with Emma is in its early stages, it provokes a revealing dispute between Mr Knightley and Mrs Weston.

Although Mrs Weston has "'been seeing their intimacy with the greatest pleasure'", she is not long surprised by Mr Knightley's insistent disapproval. She calls the past to our attention[3] by remarking, "'This will certainly be the beginning of one of our quarrels about Emma'"; and she is well able to "'imagine [his] objection to Harriet Smith. She is not the superior young woman which Emma's friend ought to be'" (36). For both of them, Harriet herself is a minor consideration. Mr Knightley considers that, through Emma's flighty influence, she may form ideas above her dubious station. Mrs Weston gradually yields much of this ground. Unlike Mr Knightley, she is slow to judge a girl she hardly knows; and her faith in Emma supplies her chief point of resistance.

On the major issue, the question of Harriet's possible influence on Emma, Mrs Weston seems at first to be neglecting everything but Emma's immediate need for a companion. To Mr Knightley such needs are trifling beside his dread that Emma will be harmed by the "'hourly flattery'" (38) of Harriet's ignorance. By repeatedly over-ruling Mrs Weston's gentle attempts to change the subject, he drives her at last into the open. Her real premise, which she had never expected to have questioned, is her confidence in Emma's "'good sense'" (39). And, having stated it, she changes the subject once again.

Although Mr Knightley finally agrees not to "'plague [her] any more'", he cannot resist a parting shot: "'Emma shall be an angel, and I will keep my spleen to myself till Christmas brings John and Isabella. John loves Emma with a reasonable and therefore not a

3. Professor L. C. Knights has rightly taught us not to ask, 'How many children had Lady Macbeth?', not to pursue the lives of literary characters beyond the confines of the work in which they have their only being. But when the work itself reaches, as it were, beyond its own confines, it is not for us to draw more narrow boundaries.

blind affection'" (40). Concerned only for Emma's happiness, Mrs Weston urges him to keep his "spleen" even from his brother. Yet we should notice that, not for the last time, Mr Knightley has been seeking advantage by over-stating his opponent's claim. So far from calling Emma an angel, so far from expressing a blind affection, she has not only granted the existence of "'dear Emma's little faults'" (39)—strong words for Mrs Weston—but has even admitted that they would have seemed more trying before they were softened by fond memories of her old life at Hartfield.

When our chief witnesses disagree so radically, we must inspect their motives. They are at one, of course, in their awareness that Emma has much to learn of life. But the intensity of Mr Knightley's anxiety springs from feelings that even he does not yet understand. He knows that he has "'a very sincere interest in Emma'"(40), that he does "'love to look at her'" (39), and even—in an ironical foreshadowing of the ball at the Crown Inn—that "'Isabella does not seem more my sister'" (40). But his determination to be rational reveals much more than he knows. Why must he openly qualify his appreciation of Emma's beauty by confessing to being "'a partial old friend'" (39)? Why those strenuous efforts to remain reasonable and not blind in his affection? Why must he have "'no . . . charm thrown over [his] senses'" (37)? In no other connection does his customary good sense require such conscious self-command.

During this very dispute with Mrs Weston, Mr Knightley's underlying feelings come momentarily towards the surface. Spared, by a happy accident of history, from the dark Freudian broodings of Professor Mudrick,[4] Mr Knightley believes that Emma's intention of never marrying "'means just nothing at all'". She has simply never "'seen a man she cared for'". And he goes on to suggest, a little severely, that he would "'like to see Emma in love, and in some doubt of a return; it would do her good. But there is nobody hereabouts to attach her; and she goes so seldom from home.'" Mrs Weston is quick to agree about the lack of local suitors, her purpose being to "conceal some favourite thoughts of her own and Mr. Weston's . . . respecting Emma's destiny". Accordingly Mr Knightley's "quiet transition", "soon afterwards", to talk of the weather "convinced her that he had nothing more to say or surmise about Hartfield" (41).

These closing phrases represent the impersonal narrator's one real intervention in all this chapter; and when Jane Austen's narrator suddenly intervenes to distinguish between a saying and a surmising or to remark that someone is "convinced" of something,

4. Marvin Mudrick, *Jane Austen: Irony as Defense and Discovery*, pp. 192, 203.

we should be brought to the alert. Mr Knightley's unexpected interest in the weather seems, therefore, to imply that Mrs Weston's conviction is unfounded and that he is left with more to surmise about Hartfield than he cares to say. But such fleeting glimpses of his underlying love for Emma only confirm him, for a long time to come, in his dissatisfaction with her as she is. Quite overlooking the difference between her age and his, he solemnly complains, for example, that Emma "'will never submit to any thing requiring industry and patience, and a subjection of the fancy to the understanding'" (37). Perhaps we can allow Emma the last word on this occasion. After telling Harriet that "'Mr. Knightley's downright, decided, commanding sort of manner . . . suits *him* very well'", she adds that "'if any young man were to set about copying him, he would not be sufferable'" (34). She might almost be prescribing for herself.

Those "favourite thoughts" of the Westons, meanwhile, are of a possible attachment between Emma and Frank Churchill. It is a natural impulse: but, since Mrs Weston has never even met her step-son, it is fanciful enough to remind us not to let her replace Mr Knightley as spokesman for the author. By the same token, her gentle meliorism, well attuned to Emma at her present age, must formerly have smacked of *laissez-faire*:

"... ever since she was twelve, Emma has been mistress of the house and of you all. In her mother she lost the only person able to cope with her. ... You might not give Emma such a complete education as your powers would seem to promise; but you were receiving a very good education from *her*, on the very material matrimonial point of submitting your own will, and doing as you were bid." (37-8)

Mr Knightley's good humour here does not disguise his bluntness: but we must accept his opinion of Miss Taylor's tutelage, confirmed as it is by the opening paragraphs of the novel.

While they ponder her future, the mistress of them all is busily extending her sway. Her own boredom and Harriet's particular style of beauty first attract Emma. The success of their first evening together persuades her that "a Harriet Smith, therefore, one whom she could summon at any time to a walk, would be a valuable addition to her privileges . . . exactly the something which her home required" (26). The attitude implied in "*a* Harriet Smith" and "exactly the something" long governs their relationship. Although she would wish to regard Harriet's admiration as evidence of good sense, Emma soon accepts that "strength of understanding must not be expected". Swiftly resigning her hope of a real friend, a true substitute for Mrs Weston, Emma makes do with a humble minion whose only desire is "to be guided by any one she looked up to" (26). And at least Harriet's doubtful birth must promise a romantic mystery.

Emma's despotism is only too benevolent: "Harriet would be loved as one to whom she could be useful. . . . Her first attempts at usefulness were in an endeavour to find out who were the parents" (26-7). Upon the complete failure of these inquiries, "Emma was obliged to fancy what she liked" (27). Her fanciful hopes induce her to detach Harriet from "the inferior society of Highbury and its connections" (23). For, so she insists, "'There can be no doubt of your being a gentleman's daughter, and you must support your claim to that station by every thing within your own power, or there will be plenty of people who would take pleasure in degrading you'" (30). How better to support Harriet's claims than by finding her a suitable husband? And who more suitable than Mr Elton? He is "quite the gentleman himself, and without low connections; at the same time not of any family that could fairly object to the doubtful birth of Harriet". And, besides seeing in him "a young man whom any woman not fastidious might like" (35), has she not already decided to find him a wife?

Emma's notion that Harriet is of gentle birth exerts a potent influence on her treatment of the Martins, the friends with whom Harriet has spent the summer lately ended. She sees Robert Martin especially as an obstacle to Harriet's match with Elton. Certainly Emma knows the Martins only "by character" (23) in the archaic sense of general repute;[5] and what she has heard extorts a reluctant approval. They are "very good sort of people", living "very creditably she believed". Yet they "must be doing her harm" because they "must be coarse and unpolished, and very unfit to be the intimates of a girl who wanted only a little more knowledge and elegance to be quite perfect" (23). For her own part, she tells Harriet, "'The yeomanry are precisely the order of people with whom I feel I can have nothing to do. A degree or two lower, and a creditable appearance might interest me'" (29).

Most modern critics take Emma's attitude to the Martins, and this last passage especially, as leading evidence of an outrageous social snobbery. Some, indeed, regard snobbery as her predominant characteristic, and are quite overcome by democratic zeal:

Emma is the heroine of this novel only in the sense that she is its principal character and that it is through her consciousness that the situations are

---

5. *The Oxford English Dictionary* (*See* 'character', 13): 'The estimate formed of a person's qualities; reputation: when used without qualifying epithet implying "favourable estimate, good repute".' *See also* Mrs Croft's remark to her husband, " 'I had known you by character, however, long before' " (*Persuasion*, p. 92).

revealed; she is no heroine in the conventional sense. She is not merely spoilt and selfish, she is snobbish and proud, and her snobbery leads her to inflict suffering that might ruin happiness. She has, until her experience and her feeling for Mr. Knightley brings [sic] her to a fuller, more humane understanding, an attitude to marriage typical of the ruling class. She sees human relationships in terms of class snobbery and property qualifications.[6]

Neither 'snob' nor 'snobbery' seems to have been used in Jane Austen's day. And those senses to which Thackeray first gave general currency, the *only* relevant senses recognized by *The Oxford English Dictionary*, are already archaic. In the short space of a hundred years, the words have lost their bearing on the vulgar aspirations of men of mean birth. *The Shorter Oxford English Dictionary* approaches modern usage more nearly, defining a snob as 'one whose ideas and conduct are prompted by a vulgar admiration for wealth or social position'. Setting aside its Thackerayan overtones, we can make do with this definition. The question, I take it, is whether Emma's ideas and conduct are prompted by an improper emphasis on her own wealth and social position.

Only in the eyes of a more fervent, modern egalitarian than Jane Austen could conceivably have been is it snobbery to acknowledge that social differences exist. Mrs Weston (400) and Mr Knightley (428) both recognize that, in point of birth, Jane Fairfax is not Frank Churchill's equal. They know her personal virtues but do not ignore the prescripts of society. And, ignorant as he is of Harriet's birth, Mr Knightley declares that, through Emma's influence, such a girl "'will grow just refined enough to be uncomfortable with those among whom birth and circumstances have placed her home'" (38). But life in Highbury usually permits differences of rank to be taken for granted. Both the Knightleys and the Woodhouses can rest quietly in their primacy. And, if Mr Knightley is more consistently charitable than Emma, Emma still has her moments of active charity and better appreciates what charity entails (86-7) than do such Dickensian paragons as John Jarndyce.

Yet Emma is far more given than Mr Knightley to outbursts of anger and dislike. And on these occasions she often relies on the easy language of snobbery rather than search into her own real motives. The Coxe sisters, she tells Harriet, "'are, without exception, the most vulgar girls in Highbury'" (233). The uncle who had cared for Augusta Hawkins can only be "the drudge of some attorney, and too stupid to rise" (183). Miss Nash may well be satisfied with her sister's marriage to a linen-draper: "'One should

6. Arnold Kettle, '*Emma*' in Ian Watt (ed.), *Jane Austen*, p. 116.

be sorry to see greater pride or refinement in the teacher of a school'"
(56). The Coles, no doubt, "were very respectable in their way, but
they ought to be taught that it was not for them to arrange the
terms on which the superior families would visit them" (207). And
Emma tells herself that her dislike of visiting the Bateses stems from
"the horror of being in danger of falling in with the second rate and
third rate of Highbury, who were calling on them for ever" (155).

In these vigorous expressions of the least attractive side of her
nature, Emma certainly takes aid and comfort from her superior
social position. To acknowledge this, however, is by no means to
accept that, as the dictionary has it, her ideas and conduct are
prompted by social considerations. In most such instances, Emma is
striking back against what she regards as an attack. The Coxe
sisters, Miss Nash, and Augusta Hawkins all interfere with her
precious plans for Harriet. Her puzzled dislike for the Bateses, as we
shall see in due course, springs from deeper and more obscure
motives. Her attitude to the Coles alone approaches snobbery,
properly so called. With them, however, Emma is prompted not
even by dislike but by an absurdly overweening sense of her *duty* to
society. Her tone is not that of a Lady Catherine de Bourgh but
that of many a Tory gentlewoman, speaking more in sorrow than
in anger and delighted to find, when she does condescend to visit
them, that she need not "repent her condescension" (231). Jane
Austen's gentle and amused mockery of these pretensions sharply
distinguishes Emma from Lady Catherine: "She must have delighted the Coles—worthy people, who deserved to be made happy!
—And left a name behind her that would not soon die away" (231).

Sir Walter Elliot despises his neighbours simply because they are
his social inferiors, and makes no exceptions save partially for
toadies like old Shepherd and Mrs Clay. Emma, some might argue,
makes a similar exception for Harriet Smith. But, without any hint
of servility, others of her 'inferiors' like Mrs Weston and Mrs
Goddard rank high in her esteem. Emma's strictures, unlike Sir
Walter's, are not prompted by social considerations: those considerations merely offer her a ready-made vocabulary for expressing her
wrath, whatever its real basis. The difference explains why Emma
is able at last to cast off her 'snobbery' so swiftly and completely.
Unlike Sir Walter Elliot, she needs only a sharp lesson to remind
her that even those whom she dislikes are individuals in their own
right: to remind her, for instance, that there are better ways of
attacking Mrs Elton than through the accident of her uncle's
occupation.

Returning to the Martins, we find once more that Emma's
disapproval is couched in social terms: "They must be coarse and

unpolished, and very unfit to be the intimates of a girl who . . .". Everything hinges on the phrase, "a girl who . . .". Emma's great object is to assist a social ugly duckling to discover its swanhood. And, not yet properly appreciating Elton's personal deficiencies, she hopes to enlist him in her cause. Accordingly she finds it necessary to resist the claims of the Martin family and of Robert in particular. Granted her premise about Harriet, there is a formidable logic about her proceedings.

But should we grant a premise rejected at once by Mr Knightley and ultimately to be refuted by events? In such a case, of course, the truth, which nobody then knows, cannot be the sole consideration. Knowing Harriet as little as Emma knows the Martins, Mr Knightley defends Robert Martin by arguing that "'My only scruple in advising the match was on his account, as being beneath his deserts, and a bad connexion for him'" (61). The essential difference between Emma and Mr Knightley in this affair lies in her youthful pride in her own judgement, her willingness to ride rough-shod over anyone, Mr Knightley not excepted, who resists her darling schemes. The years have taught Mr Knightley a sort of wisdom. Even though he thinks the match unsuitable, he is too prudent to stand between Robert Martin and his desire. Even though he disapproves of Harriet, he is content simply to avoid conversation with her. And, even though he is too sure of himself, he can argue, not unjustly, that ugly ducklings have a dreadful propensity for growing into ugly ducks. In the long run, he needs only to modify his opinion of Harriet whereas Emma, who has translated her errors into vigorous match-making and match-breaking, is left to face the damage and to experience remorse.

To see Emma's 'snobbery' in context, then, is not to condone her meddling in the lives of her fellows but only to see that it is nothing so uninteresting as snobbery. Even her grandiose generalization about the yeomanry as an order of people with whom she can have nothing to do serves not as a decisive instance of her snobbery but as one tactic among many in a campaign to steer Harriet away from Robert Martin. It is, in effect, a threat to deprive Harriet Martin, the yeoman's wife, of her friendship. She has previously assaulted Robert Martin's literacy and his good looks; she will go on to question his being of an age to marry, his financial independence, and—a brilliant stroke—the advisability of Harriet's being friendly with whoever he should marry. And all this time she is not only displaying her ignorance of the yeomanry but also fighting against a growing awareness of his personal merits. The penultimate irony is that this brilliantly conducted campaign dissipates itself in the intellectual desert of Miss Smith, who is conscious only that he has forgotten a book and that he writes a short letter. The last irony of all is that Emma will eventually be saved from her own engines only by Harriet's possessing, as Dr Craik neatly puts it, a 'mind that never opposes an argument, but is never really swayed from its own original opinion'.[7]

During Harriet's early days at Hartfield, however, there is little sign of these unamenable depths. And, ignorant as she is of Robert Martin, Emma does not reckon on *his* proving very determined. She can pause, therefore, to consider the unexpected merits of his letter of proposal:

Emma was not sorry to be pressed. She read, and was surprized. The style of the letter was much above her expectation. There were not merely no grammatical errors, but as a composition it would not have disgraced a gentleman; the language, though plain, was strong and unaffected, and the sentiments it conveyed very much to the credit of the writer. It was short, but expressed good sense, warm attachment, liberality, propriety, even delicacy of feeling. She paused over it, while Harriet stood anxiously watching for her opinion, with a "Well, well," and was at last forced to add, "Is it a good letter? or is it too short?"

"Yes, indeed, a very good letter," replied Emma rather slowly—"so good a letter, Harriet, that every thing considered, I think one of his sisters must have helped him. I can hardly imagine the young man whom I saw talking with you the other day could express himself so well, if left quite to his own powers, and yet it is not the style of a woman; no, certainly, it is too strong and concise; not diffuse enough for a woman. No doubt he is a sensible man, and I suppose may have a natural talent for—thinks strongly and clearly—and when he takes a pen in hand, his thoughts naturally find proper words. It is so with some men. Yes, I understand the sort of mind. Vigorous, decided, with sentiments to a certain point, not coarse. A better written letter, Harriet, (returning it,) than I had expected."

"Well," said the still waiting Harriet;—"well—and—and what shall I do?"

"What shall you do! In what respect? Do you mean with regard to this letter?" (50-1)

It might be argued that the first of these paragraphs delivers the narrator's judgement of the letter, against which Emma's opinion is then set. Certainly the middle sentences are those of any educated person of the time, as for instance in the well-tried distinction between language and sentiments and in established terms like "good sense" and "liberality". Yet the fact that these sentences are enclosed by phrases betokening Emma's presence, phrases like "above her expectation" and "She paused over it", suggests another relationship between the two paragraphs. The first, I submit,

7. W. A. Craik, *Jane Austen: The Six Novels*, p. 144.

expresses Emma's own unspoken opinion of the letter while the second, among other things, delivers her verdict to Harriet: and the close relationship between the two paragraphs affords an uncommonly favourable opportunity for watching Emma's mind at work.

As the first paragraph shows, the letter itself quickly gains Emma's approval. Nor can her later hesitations be attributed to Harriet's presence: for Harriet's benefit she need only have agreed that the letter was too short; and, when she does issue her verdict, she has no difficulty in expressing the exact truth in the subtly pejorative tones that her purpose requires ("'with sentiments to a certain point, not coarse'"; "'A better written letter ... than I had expected'").

Emma's real grounds for hesitation lie in the disparity between 'her' Robert Martin and his letter, in the irruption of unruly fact into her tidy little world. She can tell Harriet anything she pleases, but she cannot disguise from herself the merits of the letter or persist in telling herself that it is his sister's work. For a moment she is genuinely puzzled—but she soon persuades herself that she can "understand the sort of mind" and returns to the simpler task of managing Harriet.

The brief interval is crucial in that Emma, who knows hardly any man, satisfies herself with a remarkable generalization: "'It is so with some men'". Dr Chapman notes (491-2) half a dozen occasions when Mr Knightley comes into Emma's mind, unbidden and unrecognized, as a criterion of what a man should be. This is another of them. The Knightleys excepted, no man of Emma's acquaintance remotely matches the terms she chooses here and, as we have begun to see, the phrase "a sensible man" has a peculiar force in *Emma*. She is not, of course, fully identifying Robert Martin with Mr Knightley: she keeps the identification within bounds by twice glancing at the old distinction between 'nature' and 'nurture', making Robert Martin into a sort of rustic Knightley, a prince of yeomen but a yeoman still. Her difficulty in concealing Robert Martin's merits from herself is growing stronger. Yet she holds unshaken to her plans for Harriet and pursues them with unabated zest: "'Do you mean with regard to this letter?'"

Robert Martin's surprising powers of composition have been transformed from a threat to Emma's governance into a positive tribute to her analytic genius. His proposal of marriage is rapidly disposed of and Emma sees no further obstacle in the path she has chosen for Harriet. Naturally Harriet will have her moments of irrational regret: but time and Mr Elton will attend to these. Miss Woodhouse has given her little senate laws and now sits attentive to her own applause. In this applause, as much as anywhere, the comic tone sustained throughout the whole affair is to be felt. We are simply not allowed to take Emma as seriously as she takes herself when, for instance, she shuts her new discoveries about Robert Martin quite out of her mind: "it would be a small consolation to her, for the clownish manner which might be offending her every hour of the day, to know that her husband could write a good letter" (55).

Emma's celebrations are cut short next morning when Mr Knightley comes, poor man, to tell her of her little friend's good fortune. On learning of the refusal and on guessing its real author, he grows "red with surprize and displeasure" and stands above Emma "in tall indignation" (60). Although he has the better of the ensuing quarrel, his advantage does not lie in any point of principle. For Emma, a gentleman's daughter has refused a farmer: for Mr Knightley, a "'gentleman-farmer'" (62) has been refused by "'the natural daughter of nobody knows whom, with probably no settled provision at all, and certainly no respectable relations'" (61).

To the extent that their disagreement hinges on the facts of Harriet's birth, Mr Knightley is still at no advantage. They are both obliged to deal only in loose inferences from Harriet's present situation; and, throughout this chapter, they both gloss over their ignorance by referring continually to what each regards as "probable". There are occasions, of course, when we must all deal in such inferences. But Jane Austen well knows that, when we grow dogmatic, events are likely to defy us. The behaviour of Marianne Dashwood, Henry Crawford, Frank Churchill and Jane Fairfax quite escapes the calculations of their fellows. And, if General Tilney is not the Italianate monster of Catherine's wilder imaginings, he still cannot be understood in terms of that easy "'sense of the probable'" (*Northanger Abbey*, p. 197) which his son so confidently recommends. When Emma decides what Robert Martin is probably like, his letter arrives to confound her. When Mr Knightley erects a laborious set of inferences to prove that Robert Martin will propose that day, his protégé has already defeated his logic. And when the truth of Harriet's birth is discovered at last, she is neither the lost princess of Emma's imaginings nor the lowly pauper of Mr Knightley's. It is fitting, therefore, that the present dispute should end in a comparison unflattering to both contenders. Certainly Emma is not "so absolutely satisfied with herself, so entirely convinced that her opinions were right and her adversary's wrong, as Mr. Knightley" (67). Yet her frivolous treatment of serious issues is shown in the very speed of her recovery: "a little time and the return of Harriet were very adequate restoratives" (67).

After all such allowances are made, Mr Knightley still retains a clear advantage, which stems above all from his steady emphasis on the personal qualities of the couple themselves: on the good nature they both display; on Robert Martin's being the possessor of those "'good hands'" (58, 61) in which Harriet might prosper (and in the mention of which Emma had thought to find a compliment); on his good sense and Harriet's lack of it; and on his being too modest to have proposed marriage without encouragement. Emma, meanwhile, is no such fool as to challenge him on Robert Martin's personal merits and is obliged to make what she can of Harriet. Harriet's good sense does not carry her far: "'She is not a clever girl, but she has better sense than you are aware of'" (63). She argues for Harriet's amiability in terms that Mr Knightley will eventually learn to accept. She has always admired Harriet's beauty —but her superlatives flow ever more freely as her present need increases.

Emma tacitly admits the flimsiness of her case by making several abortive attempts to change the subject and, still more plainly, by borrowing from Mr Knightley himself a form of argument that operates without visible means of support. Throughout the novel, Mr Knightley is accustomed not only to base arguments directly on general premises but also to state his premises quite explicitly in the form of little aphorisms: in the very first chapter, he declares what may be expected of "'a straight-forward, open-hearted man ... and a rational unaffected woman'" (13) or, again, of "'a man of six or seven-and-twenty'" (14); in a later dispute there are six examples in three pages (145-7). This Johnsonian habit of mind gains its force from, but does not obviously display, a man's essential grasp of his experience. Now Mr Knightley is no second Johnson: the blunt edge of some of his aphorisms will occupy us at a later stage. But their solidity still distinguishes them from Emma's hopeful imitations:

"Oh! to be sure," cried Emma, "it is always incomprehensible to a man that a woman should ever refuse an offer of marriage. A man always imagines a woman to be ready for anybody who asks her."
"Nonsense! a man does not imagine any such thing." (60)

From first to last, then, Emma must chiefly rely on her belief that Harriet is of gentle birth. And yet, as she rings that little tune through all its changes, one begins to ask why she *needs* to champion Harriet so insistently. So far as an answer can be localized, it lies, I consider, in a comment by Professor Trilling:

... many of her wrong judgments and actions are directed to a very engaging end, a very right purpose. She believes in her own distinction and vividness and she wants all around her to be distinguished and vivid. It is indeed

32

unpardonable arrogance, as she comes to see, that she should undertake to arrange Harriet Smith's destiny, that she plans to "form" Harriet, making her, as it were, the mere material or stuff of a creative act. Yet the destiny is not meanly conceived, the act is meant to be truly creative—she wants Harriet to be a distinguished and not a commonplace person, she wants nothing to be commonplace, she requires of life that it be well shaped and impressive, and alive.[8]

These qualities are especially apparent in a splendid passage (62) where Emma argues that Harriet is a gentleman's daughter because she associates with gentlemen's daughters—or, at any rate, with one. The same passage, however, suggests an additional ground for her fervour. Miss Woodhouse may present an assured face to the world; but there are times when it can scarcely mask Emma's grave impulses of doubt. In this instance, one senses a growing need to conceal, above all from herself, that Harriet is *personally* unworthy of her friendship, that Harriet's chief claim on her is that she has been allowed to establish such a claim. It is, in very truth, a question of the sphere in which Harriet moves.

Arrogance; creativity; the brazening over of half-conscious doubts: they will all take new forms in new contexts as Emma's career proceeds. Yet it would be wrong to single out this moment and these qualities too emphatically, to cry, 'Here! Here is the *real* Emma!' She originally took up Harriet rather arbitrarily. Her interest has already been sustained beyond its natural limits by the romantic mystery of Harriet's birth, the campaign against Robert Martin, the chance of defying Mr Knightley, and the managing of Mr Elton. When success on this last point seems within easy reach, the impending arrival of her sister quite supplants her concern for the "lovers" and she "hardly wished to have more leisure for them. There are people, who the more you do for them, the less they will do for themselves" (91). A little later, however, her interest is sharply restored by her need to repair the damage she has done to Harriet. And, later again, new motives will arise.

The immediate dispute seems likely to end in a complete *impasse* when Emma makes a sad blunder. All other claims aside, she remarks, Harriet has recently learnt what gentlemen are; and now, undoubtedly, "'nothing but a gentleman in education and manner has any chance with Harriet'" (65). After a little thought, Mr Knightley takes the point and warns Emma that Mr Elton "'does not mean to throw himself away'" (66). Some have instanced this warning as a mark of Mr Knightley's extreme acuteness. But Emma's

8. Lionel Trilling, '*Emma* and the Legend of Jane Austen' in *Beyond Culture: Essays on Literature and Learning*, p. 45.

preceding remarks give clues enough; there has been gossip already (56, 176) about Mr Elton's visits to Hartfield; and Mr Knightley could never suppose that Emma herself is drawn to Elton. At all events, Emma disclaims any such plan and Mr Knightley wishes her a curt good-morning, disappointed for Robert Martin, mortified at having encouraged him, and exceedingly provoked by Emma's part in the affair. Upon his departure, Emma is left in a mood of doubt and introspection which soon turns into a stout re-affirmation of her belief in Mr Elton's attachment to Harriet.

III

Jane Austen manages the whole phase of the novel concerning Emma, Harriet, and Mr Elton so delicately that it is easy to over-look the difficulties she has met. The essential problem is that, for all Emma's attention to Mr Elton's behaviour, she must be utterly deceived: capable of approving—if only as *Harriet's* suitor—of a man who will prove a worthy mate for the charming Augusta Hawkins; blind to his true intentions; unaware of the encourage-ments given him by her own words and actions; and yet, for all this catalogue of folly, deceived in such a way that she does not seem merely a fool. These hard conditions would no doubt be met if she were the victim of a freakish concatenation of events: but then the whole affair, a mere comedy of errors, would have no place in a novel concerned always with expressive incidents and meaningful behaviour. Again, Emma might pardonably be deceived by the Joseph Surface of a Highbury intrigue. Such an Elton, however, would not only take our chief attention away from Emma but would also pre-empt Frank Churchill's role. He would, worse still, destroy his own prime function, his paving of the way for later episodes by enabling us to see that, given a suitable occasion, Emma can deceive herself with little or no help. In place of all such neat, unsatisfactory solutions, Jane Austen treads a long and narrow path, working by indirections towards a distant goal. The result transforms the material of a comedy of errors as completely as the affairs of Frank Churchill afterwards transform the material of a comedy of intrigue.

Her certainty that she can follow such a path declares itself from the outset in her willingness to hide nothing from the reader. When Mr Elton is first mentioned (13-14), Mr Knightley is warning Emma that such a man will find a wife for himself. He is next heard of in a seemingly artless comment by the narrator:

Real, long-standing regard brought the Westons and Mr. Knightley; and by Mr. Elton, a young man living alone without liking it, the privilege of exchanging any vacant evening of his own blank solitude for the elegancies

34

and society of Mr. Woodhouse's drawing-room and the smiles of his lovely daughter, was in no danger of being thrown away. (20)

His need for a wife, echoing and re-echoing in "alone", "vacant", "blank", and "solitude", is neatly juxtaposed with his interest in Hartfield. The language that defines his motives already smacks of the circulating library of the day, of a hundred novels where "elegancies" are mere trumperies, where "society" is a congeries of drawing-room gossips, and where the smiles of a lovely daughter are no more than the oglings and simperings of stale coquettes like Anne Steele and Isabella Thorpe. On the few occasions when, instead of parroting the remarks of his companion of the moment, Mr Elton will venture to speak for himself, this same vacuously literary language will be the language of his choice: "'Charming Miss Woodhouse! allow me to interpret this interesting silence. It confesses that you have long understood me'"(131). His motives are further undermined, even in this early passage, by the submerged antithesis between them and the "real, long-standing regard" that brings the Westons and Mr Knightley to visit Hartfield. At the beginning of the sixth chapter, when Mr Elton himself first enters, it is upon a florid compliment, an "Exactly so!" and a series of feeble echoes. And, before he and Emma have exchanged a dozen remarks, the reader knows that the match she plans for Harriet, the match that "every body else must think of and predict" (35), will come to nothing because the charming Miss Woodhouse is herself more eligible for Hymen's saffron robe.

But Emma, thinking only of her plans and Harriet's advantage, is slow to discover that "her own behaviour to him ... [is] so complaisant and obliging" as to deceive "a man of ordinary observation and delicacy, like Mr. Elton" (136). Only after the event can she appreciate the ambiguity of her exaggerated courtesies: "'Well, if you give me such kind encouragement, Mr. Elton, I believe I shall try what I can do'" (43-4); "'I did ... forswear ever drawing anybody again. But for Harriet's sake, or rather for my own, and as there are no husbands and wives in the case at present, I will break my resolution now'" (46).

Given such encouragements, he naturally interprets those other moments when Miss Woodhouse steps back behind Miss Smith as revealing just the dreadful coyness an Elton would expect. With what becoming modesty does she praise her little friend's beauty, with no thought for the pleasing talent exercised in painting it! With what a pretty mixture of ardour and timidity does she gain entry into the vicarage only to take refuge in the bosom of his housekeeper, leaving him to make conversation with Miss Smith!

And with what amiable solicitude does she offer to give up a whole evening of his company, lest a cold journey should injure his health!

His last doubts must have ceased when he saw how the "'little effusion'" (82), which he had passed off—so tritely and transparently —as a friend's, was received at Hartfield. When Miss Woodhouse (who had actually sought only to spare Harriet's blushes) told him that she herself had copied out this particular charade, he examined the book "very attentively" and then summoned all his powers of speech:

> "I have no hesitation in saying," replied Mr. Elton, though hesitating a good deal while he spoke, "I have no hesitation in saying—at least if my friend feels at all as *I* do—I have not the smallest doubt that, could he see his little effusion honoured as *I* see it, (looking at the book again, and replacing it on the table,) he would consider it as the proudest moment of his life." (82)

Through all those weeks of autumn and early winter, while Elton's hopes are rising, Emma is congratulating herself on the progress of her second essay in match-making: "'the state of his mind is as clear and decided, as my wishes on the subject have been ever since I knew you'" (73). She meanwhile finds a little private amusement in his affected ways: "'it will be an "Exactly so," as he says himself'" (49); there is "a sort of parade in his speeches which was very apt to incline her to laugh" (82). Though Emma, of all people, can ill afford to laugh, it is time to consider how her folly is extenuated.

In the first place, Emma has none of our privileged access to the novelist's ironies. In tones that echo the beginning of the novel, the narrator opens the sixth and ninth chapters by drawing our attention to points on which Emma "could not feel a doubt" (42), matters of which "she was quite convinced" (42), "plans and proceedings [which] were more and more justified, and endeared to her by the general appearances of the next few days" (69). It is one thing for her to be warned by the brothers Knightley; quite another for us to be instructed by an omniscient narrator.

Again, her folly is mitigated by what one might call the malleability of Mr Elton's speech. Much of what he says—his echoings, his clichés, his catch-phrases—*says* nothing but only implies a vague complaisance. To Emma, who is accustomed to the direct and precise speech of Mr Knightley and Mrs Weston, the task of discovering a meaning in Mr Elton's leaden-footed arabesques must seem too unpromising to entertain, and she is almost obliged to impose a meaning all her own. Jane Austen is careful, moreover, to prevent Emma from attending at times when Mr Elton does make himself more plain.[9] There is one such moment in the famous passage where the company assembled delivers judgement on the portrait. Mr Woodhouse is gravely concerned for Harriet, who is shown as out of doors with only a little shawl over her shoulders, and he remains quite unmoved by their appeals to the fine weather. Mr Knightley, no respecter of artistic licence, insists that Emma has made her too tall.[10] And Emma, who will never admit to *him* that she has consciously improved on nature (cf. 47), is so attentive to his verdict that she hears nothing of another conversation. "Not in the least suspecting that she was addressing a lover" (47), Mrs Weston quietly tells Mr Elton that the portrait flatters Miss Smith's eye-brows and eyelashes. But where Emma would have expected a ballad made to that questionable eye-brow, Elton instead defends the likeness and quite neglects Miss Smith.

"Not in the least suspecting that she was addressing a lover": even so late as the dinner-party at Randalls, Mrs Weston can be surprised by a first glimpse of Mr Elton's real intentions (125). Since she remains ignorant for so long, our sense of Emma's folly is further alleviated. In view of the Knightleys' swift insight into Elton's motives, it is an alleviation of particular importance, reminding us that they have opportunities denied to others. Through having heard Elton "'in unreserved moments, when there are only men present'" (66), moments when he "'can be rational and unaffected'" (111), both brothers can see the more easily behind the sentimental mask of one whose "'every feature works'" (111).

It might be argued that Emma should have heeded good advice. But who has ever done so? And, indeed, that advice is given by just those persons whose wisdom she loves to flout. Both of George Knightley's warnings about Elton are handed down to Emma, *ex cathedra*, at times when the two of them are already quarrelling. And though John Knightley finds a better opportunity, his heavy manner costs him that advantage and leaves Emma "amusing herself in the consideration of the blunders which often arise from a partial knowledge of circumstances, of the mistakes which people of high pretensions to judgment are for ever falling into" (112). When she

9. Only Henry James, I believe, can match Jane Austen's mastery of those many, quite ordinary situations where more goes on than anyone present is aware. Consider, for example, how Emma and Harriet differ about certain details of Elton's courtship (338-40).
10. This small token of large differences resembles the well-known passage in *Mansfield Park* where Edmund and Mary disagree about times and distances. It is usual to suggest that, in both cases, the man's sober view is held up for our approval; but I would argue that this interpretation is too solemn, that there is room, in both cases, for a little "feminine lawlessness" (*Mansfield Park*, p. 94).

learns that all the blunders have been her own, she is struck also by the "dreadfully mortifying" thought that "there was no denying that those brothers had penetration" (135). In thinking of them so promptly and in choosing the reluctant phrase of one who would still deny their penetration if she could, she shows how keenly she had wished to prove the superiority of her own judgement, the erroneousness of all their good advice. This closely woven relationship between Emma's dealings with Mr Elton and her prior attitude to the Knightleys lies nearer the heart of the matter than the alleviating circumstances previously described. For Jane Austen's course consists above all in defining Emma's motives so exactly that we recognize that, without *being* a fool, Emma can—even must—behave very foolishly in this and similar affairs.

At the height of this first serious discomfiture, Emma tries to account for her failure to grasp Mr Elton's intentions:

She looked back as well as she could; but it was all confusion. She had taken up the idea, she supposed, and made every thing bend to it. His manners, however, must have been unmarked, wavering, dubious, or she could not have been so misled. . . .

Certainly she had often, especially of late, thought his manners to herself unnecessarily gallant; but it had passed as his way, as a mere error of judgment, of knowledge, of taste. . .; but, till this very day, she had never, for an instant, suspected it to mean any thing but grateful respect to her as Harriet's friend. (134-5)

The outstanding point here lies in the second sentence, where she sees how obstinately she has wrenched her—unfailingly accurate—observations into a distorted pattern.

Yet Emma's diagnosis does not go deep enough. Its shortcomings are reflected, first of all, in the attitude she now takes to Elton's way of showing his ardour. In remarking his insincerity, she still does not see that his behaviour and her own conception of love had been in close accord, that his sighs, for example, and her comments on them had been inspired by the same weary muse of literary romance. He had spoken "with a sort of sighing animation, which had a vast deal of the lover" (43). He "sighed out his half sentences of admiration just as he ought" (69). He was, "as she could perceive, most earnestly careful that nothing ungallant, nothing that did not breathe a compliment to the sex should pass his lips" (70). And, again, "he sighed and smiled himself off in a way that left the balance of approbation much in his favour" (111). Though Emma smiles sometimes at these affectations, even her doubts reflect the same assumptions about love: "This was very proper; the sigh which accompanied it was really estimable; but it should have lasted longer" (115). In mistaking the object of his attentions, she has only confused one sentimental hero with another (as anyone might do!). She has supposed, as it were, that he was playing Orville to Harriet's Evelina, never dreaming that this Orville was a would-be Valancourt, and she herself his Emily. Her underlying error, however, has been to suppose that sighs like these could possibly reflect "a strong passion at war with all interested motives" (67). As she looks back into the confusion of the past weeks, she draws a very pertinent distinction: "Sighs and fine words had been given in abundance; but she could hardly devise any set of expressions, or fancy any tone of voice, less allied with real love" (135). Her experience with Mr Elton has taught her something; but her understanding of "real love", a subject on which she is never loth to dogmatize, will long remain too limited to distinguish justly between Mr Knightley's and Frank Churchill's behaviour towards her.

An adequate diagnosis, furthermore, might be expected to mark the beginning of other kinds of reform. Certainly Emma can now tell herself that:

It was foolish, it was wrong, to take so active a part in bringing any two people together. It was adventuring too far, assuming too much, making light of what ought to be serious, a trick of what ought to be simple. She was quite concerned and ashamed, and resolved to do such things no more. (136-7)

And yet, within moments, she finds herself mentally canvassing William Coxe as a possible suitor for Harriet—and rejecting him because he does not meet her own standards. Certainly she has the grace to blush at this swift relapse. With Robert Martin, however, she still holds her original ground: "'There I was quite right. That was well done of me; but there I should have stopped, and left the rest to time and chance'" (137).

An even more striking instance of Emma's unregeneracy lies precisely in her most strenuous essay in reform. Harriet's modest and generous reception of the news about Elton so adds to Emma's contriteness that their old intimacy is quite restored, and Emma patiently and cheerfully submits to weeks of lamentation. But, as if this were not penance enough, she must model her new self on her simple-minded, tender-hearted little friend. The sheer absurdity of this enterprise is immediately revealed and its transience fore-shadowed by the delightful flashes of unregeneracy that run through its very proposal:

. . . she listened to her and tried to console her with all her heart and under-standing—really for the time convinced that Harriet was the superior creature of the two—and that to resemble her would be more for her own welfare and happiness than all that genius or intelligence could do.

It was rather too late in the day to set about being simple-minded and ignorant; but she left her with every previous resolution confirmed of being humble and discreet, and repressing imagination all the rest of her life. (142)

IV

This last, high-flown resolution of Emma's can serve us as a cue: it is time to examine the meanings attached, in the novel as a whole, to the imagination and the associated concepts of fancy and reason. At the time when *Emma* was written, of course, these concepts were passing through a vigorous but cloudy phase of their long history. *Biographia Literaria* itself appeared in 1817, little more than a year after the publication of *Emma* and the very year of Jane Austen's death: one wonders what she would have made of Coleridge's celebrated definition of the secondary imagination. But, when even Addison's papers on the 'Pleasures of the Imagination'[11] are too theoretical to have much bearing on her usage as novelist, the century-long epistemological battles that led up to *Biographia Literaria* are scarcely to our purpose. As a repository of cultivated but unacademic usage in and beyond its author's generation, Johnson's *Dictionary* provides a better point of departure.

In the first place, Johnson cares little for the rarefied distinctions between fancy and imagination that were beginning to emerge. Although the words as he defines them are not co-extensive, they overlap enough for each to be introduced by the other as first synonym. Out of all that follows, both here and under 'reason', the second sense attributed to fancy amounts to a paradigm: 'FANCY. . . . 2. An opinion bred rather by the imagination than the reason.' In postulating so clear an antithesis between reason and imagination, Johnson takes up a firmer and simpler position than would be admitted nowadays, when the so-called 'intuitive leap' is but one example of their interpenetration. Johnson's usage differs from ours yet more sharply by virtue of his hostility towards imagination—which breeds only opinion and not knowledge. Among literary men at least, modern usage very often exhibits reason as an antiquated, though possibly noble, Augusto-Georgian ideal.[12] Imagination, on

11. *The Spectator*, Nos 411-421, 21 June-3 July 1712. Although Addison seldom adopts the jargon of empiricism, his concern is nevertheless with sense-perception, both immediate and recollected; with the associations to which it gives rise; and, above all, with attendant implications for his unoriginal aesthetics.

12. This attitude is well exemplified by Gibbon's modern critics. The best of them, like D. M. Low and G. M. Young, achieve a perceptive and sympathetic illustration—in Gibbon's own sense of the word—of his great enterprise. But the generality are content to assert that his Romans and his barbarians alike are judged by their ability to assume a periwigged rationalism.

the other hand, is frequently enshrined as 'the creative faculty of the mind in its highest aspect; the power of framing new and striking intellectual conceptions; poetic genius' (*The Oxford English Dictionary*, *see* 'imagination', 4b). Whatever the merits of this position, its difference from Johnson is plain. In order to illustrate his leading definition of 'reason', Johnson turns at once to Hooker: '*Reason* is the director of man's will, discovering in action what is good; for the laws of well-doing are the dictates of right *reason*.' And when Johnson forsakes the quasi-objectivity of the lexicographer and turns author on his own account, 'imagination' is a frequent object of his scorn. 'Imagination' leads Rasselas on his vain pursuit of an ideal 'choice of life'. With the weight of *The Rambler* behind him, Imlac argues that the very pyramids were created 'only in compliance with that hunger of imagination which preys incessantly upon life, and must be always appeased by some employment'. In Chapter xliv—entitled, 'The dangerous prevalence of imagination'—Imlac declares:

There is no man whose imagination does not sometimes predominate over his reason, who can regulate his attention wholly by his will, and whose ideas will come and go at his command. No man will be found in whose mind airy notions do not sometimes tyrannise, and force him to hope or fear beyond the limits of sober probability. All power of fancy over reason is a degree of insanity; but . . . it is not pronounced madness but when it becomes ungovernable.[13]

Such qualifications as Johnson will admit appear when Rasselas sees how the Philosopher of Reason is driven to recant by the death of his daughter.[14] Yet, even here, the doctrine itself exhibits a power that survives the defeat of its advocate: 'He compared reason to the sun, of which the light is constant, uniform, and lasting; and fancy to a meteor, of bright but transitory lustre, irregular in its motion, and delusive in its direction' (*Rasselas*, p. 425). And Johnson's own faith is nobly re-affirmed elsewhere, as when he insists that:

13. Samuel Johnson, *The History of Rasselas, Prince of Abissinia* (1759), Chapters xxxii and xliv. I quote throughout from Mona Wilson (ed.), *Johnson: Prose and Poetry*, London 1950, where these passages are on pp. 449, 468-9.
    Both of these famous passages are referred to by Dr F. W. Bradbrook in a brief comment on reason and imagination, as advocated by Mr Knightley and Emma respectively: *see* his *Jane Austen: 'Emma'*, pp. 49-50. The matter is carried no further in his larger work, *Jane Austen and Her Predecessors*.
14. The incident is reminiscent of the one in *Joseph Andrews* where Adams, discoursing on reason to poor Joseph, is overthrown by the reported drowning of his little son. An essentially similar, though more delicate, irony is to be seen at times in *Tom Jones*: for example, in Book I, Chapter vii.

41

The irregular combinations of fanciful invention may delight a-while, by that novelty of which the common satiety of life sends us all in quest; but the pleasures of sudden wonder are soon exhausted, and the mind can only repose on the stability of truth. (Preface to *Shakespeare*, p.491)

Though all three of the terms we are concerned with appear very frequently in Jane Austen's novels, they require delicate handling.[15] They often play only a casual part in the flow of the dialogue and ought not to be burdened with significance. Again, Jane Austen's characters speak for themselves far more vigorously than ever an Imlac does: any inference from their words to their author's meaning must therefore be most cautious.

With caution, however, certain tendencies can be established. As a noun for some such concept as right reason, "reason" itself occurs only rarely in *Emma*. And, though "reasonable" is a frequent term of approbation, it commonly means nothing more than "moderate", and appears in contexts of no special force. "A reasonable visit paid" (193), Mr Weston and his son leave Hartfield. And Mr Woodhouse is pleased to assure his friends that, at Hartfield, "'our hours are . . . reasonable'" (209). In a rarer but more significant aspect, "reason" and "reasonable" will carry us further than this. But let us turn first to "rational", which occurs quite as commonly and which is almost always used in a serious sense.[16]

Essentially it is Mr Knightley's word. He uses it almost as often as Emma even though he has much less to say. And when Emma does use the word, she often has his standards in mind. His influence may lie behind the innocent pomposity of Harriet who, on destroying her scrap of court plaster and her stump of pencil, exclaims, "'See how rational I am grown'" (338). On no other occasion is she given access to a word whose full sense clearly passes her comprehension. John Knightley asserts that, in male company, Elton can be

---

15. Since each of these words occurs, in one or another of its forms, eighty or more times in *Emma* alone, the examples to be quoted are either typical or of particular importance.

16. Johnson's *Dictionary* gives three senses, of which the second and the third clearly relate to what follows: 'RATIONAL. . . . 1. Having the power of reasoning. . . . 2. Agreeable to reason. . . . 3. Wise; judicious: as, *a* rational *man.*'
   Of many instances of "rational" in Jane Austen's other novels, one of the most interesting occurs when the narrator speaks of the regrets that "a man of sense like Henry Crawford" must feel in having "lost the woman whom he had rationally, as well as passionately loved" (*Mansfield Park*, pp. 468-9). Set beside this and other references to him as "a man of sense" and also Jane Austen's own comment on him as "a clever, pleasant man" (*Letters*, p. 378), such a use of "rational" suggests that he is less easy to dismiss than has often been supposed.

"'rational and unaffected'" (111); and Frank Churchill hopes that, having put the Eltons' treatment of Jane Fairfax out of his mind, he is become "'rational enough'" (440) to continue his long letter. For the rest, it is Mr Knightley, Emma, and the narrator who use the word to express an ideal of social conduct, of amenability to right reason. We hear much of "rational society" (422), "rational intercourse" (165), or even "the rational pleasures of an elegant society" (164), pleasures among which "quiet rational conversation" (390) ranks high and in which, unfortunately, Mr Woodhouse cannot join (7). Mr Knightley's esteem for Mrs Weston is as "'a rational unaffected woman'" (13) and his original opinion of Harriet is that, especially through Emma's influence, she will neither "'adapt herself rationally'" (39) to her situation in life nor make a "'rational companion'" (61) for Robert Martin. Even his contempt for Frank Churchill is for one who has become "'rational'" (148) only in the sense of growing up and who turns to fine words when he "'has nothing rational to urge'" (445). The word is not one that Emma much requires in the early part of the novel; but, as her esteem for her imaginative powers dwindles, she uses it freely—and uses it, above all, in self-recrimination. She looks back on the morning at Box Hill as "more totally bare of rational satisfaction . . . than any she had ever passed" (377). In the moment when she first sees "that Mr. Knightley must marry no one but herself", she also sees "how inconsiderate, how indelicate, how irrational, how unfeeling had been her conduct" (408). And when she is convinced that she has lost him to Harriet, she can yet discover a sombre hope that, "however inferior in spirit and gaiety might be the following and every future winter of her life to the past, it would yet find her more rational, more acquainted with herself, and leave her less to regret when it were gone" (423).

But the ideal has its limitations. It is scarcely "rational" for John Knightley to deliver "a rational remonstrance or sharp retort" (93) in answer to a Mr Woodhouse. And it is not only John Knightley who sees Elton as sometimes rational. Worse still, George Knightley applies the word directly to the man's mercenary aspirations: "'He knows the value of a good income as well as anybody. Elton may talk sentimentally, but he will act rationally'" (66). Through the very accuracy of his opinion, his most cherished term of approbation is debased.

As with "rational", there are moments when Jane Austen's regard for "reason" is more limited than Johnson's. When "reasonable" is used in more forceful senses than those previously described, its connotations, it is true, are mostly favourable. Upon marrying Captain Weston, Miss Churchill felt "unreasonable regrets at [her] brother's unreasonable anger" (15). Jane Fairfax deeply regrets that the strain imposed by her secret engagement has made her "'unreasonable'" (419). And Emma recognizes that to surrender, on Harriet's account, her own hopes of marriage would be "generosity run mad, opposing all that could be probable or reasonable" (431). There is a more equivocal instance when Mr Knightley tells Emma that, in asserting that men regard beauty and good temper as a woman's highest claims, she is "'abusing the reason you have'" (64). For, if Emma is suppressing part of the truth, Mr Knightley is ignoring some obvious social facts.[17] On the only other occasions when the noun itself is used in a full and serious sense, reason seems unable to stand alone. When Mrs Weston is described as addressing Emma "with a great deal of reason, and at least equal affection" (420), the narrator admits a distinction which Mr Knightley soon afterwards concedes. Wishing to console Emma for the 'loss' of Frank Churchill, believing that she is calm only by a noble effort of self-command, and summoning all his love and generosity, he urges her that, "'He is no object of regret, indeed! and it will not be very long, I hope, before that becomes the acknowledgment of more than your reason'" (426).

Just as Johnson distinguishes many senses of the word, so *Emma* displays "fancy" in various garbs, ranging from the least of erroneous suppositions to delusive notions of quite a serious kind. There is room in that wide range for the caprices of love (42, 180, 184, 267), for the whims confessed by Mr Woodhouse (10), and for the hypochondria, actual and alleged, of Mrs Churchill (317, 387).

But in its most constant area of meaning, "fancy" in *Emma*, as in *Rasselas*, concerns those airy notions that impel men to depart from nature's laws, as discovered by reason and understanding. When only Mr Knightley expounds the direct Johnsonian antithesis and when—as we have begun to see—his more oracular moments do not escape Jane Austen's irony, we may question whether nature's laws are quite as accessible as he believes. Certainly the case is not one where 'God said, "Let Knightley be!" and all was light'. The antithesis itself is made explicit when he deplores Emma's failure to "'submit to any thing requiring industry and patience, and a subjection of the fancy to the understanding'" (37). It appears again

17. Elinor Dashwood's opinion of Mr Palmer indicates that Jane Austen is well aware of those facts: "His temper might perhaps be a little soured by finding, like many others of his sex, that through some unaccountable bias in favour of beauty, he was the husband of a very silly woman,—but she knew that this kind of blunder was too common for any sensible man to be lastingly hurt by it" (*Sense and Sensibility*, p. 112).

when he suggests that, simply by agreeing with him, she can always be right, always in harmony with the dictates of nature:

"If you were as much guided by nature in your estimate of men and women, and as little under the power of fancy and whim in your dealings with them, as you are where these children are concerned, we might always think alike."

"To be sure—our discordancies must always arise from my being in the wrong."

"Yes," said he, smiling—"and reason good. I was sixteen years old when you were born." (98-9)

The time will come when he can grant Emma's right to continue in a divergent opinion (470-1). By that time, moreover, he can turn his old terms to a new purpose, as when "nature", "understanding", and "fancy" all enter into a confession that his attempts to govern her had been ill-advised and that he had exaggerated her faults (462). But by that time Emma, too, is of a different mind, with no desire to flout his advice or to force the hothouse blooms of fancy; and she replies, accordingly, that his influence had often been judicious.

It is as well that Emma, too, should change: her cult of fancy is a much more frequent source of error than any blunt antithesis. The word "fancy" is regularly used to describe amorous aspirations of which Emma happens to disapprove, as when Harriet can "dare to fancy herself the chosen of such a man" (414) as Mr Knightley or when—four times in a page—Mr Elton is said to have "fancied" himself fit for her own hand (135-6). But, though Emma is the last to see it, these fancies are less factitious than her own. For the word is one of several distinguishing marks of those many occasions when she wildly misinterprets what is before her, usually by imposing literary clichés on puzzling realities. Harriet is of unknown parentage: Emma is "obliged to fancy what she liked" (27); and she composes a suitably romantic history. Jane Fairfax's pianoforte arrives: that "very dear part of Emma, her fancy, received an amusing supply" (214); and she adds a fresh chapter to the woeful tale of Dixon's love. She meditates on the attachment between Frank Churchill and herself, "fancying interesting dialogues, and inventing elegant letters" (264). And, as soon as the real fears prompted by Mr Weston's unnatural gravity have been relieved, she readily fills in the time taken to walk to Randalls by concocting yet another wild tale: "Her fancy was very active. Half a dozen natural children, perhaps—and poor Frank cut off!" (393).

Most fittingly, she chooses the same word when she tries to make redress. In spite of some earlier gestures, Emma is slow to retract

45

her "fanciful and unfair conjectures" (384) about Jane Fairfax and to make what reparation is allowed her. So, too, when she discovers that, at bottom, she has always regarded Mr Knightley as Frank Churchill's superior and has only been "fancying" (412) otherwise. And, fearing that she has lost him to Harriet, she looks back on an earlier, less real cause of grief and recalls how he had walked in and "dissipated every melancholy fancy" (422). Much as her fancies need dissipating, however, the case is not quite absolute. At a time when she is irritated by Mr Weston's promiscuous friendliness, Emma lifts her mind above her own hurt vanity: "She liked his open manners, but a little less of open-heartedness would have made him a higher character.—General benevolence, but not general friendship, made a man what he ought to be.—She could fancy such a man" (320). Given his opinion of fancy, Mr Knightley might not care for the implied compliment: yet Emma's fancy is for once as judicious as her dormant affection is sincere.

For Jane Austen, as for both Addison and Johnson, "imagination" and "fancy" are frequently interchangeable. The whims of Mr Woodhouse and the hypochondria of Mrs Churchill are no less— or more—"imaginary" (317, 361, 387) than they are "fanciful". Several attachments are "imagined" (112, 399, 405) when they might equally well be "fancied". And the two words actually come together when Isabella transmutes the prospect of a wintry drive into an heroic struggle against the elements (127).

"Imagination" is likewise used of her sister's airy notions. Emma lets "her imagination range and work at Harriet's fortune" (69); her "imagination" (168) tells her of mischief afoot between Dixon and Jane Fairfax; and her "imagination" (206) confers on Frank Churchill the honour of being in love with her. When everyone else (except the young Knightleys) has forgotten the affair of the gypsies, it maintains its ground "in her imagination" (336) as the source of Frank Churchill's attachment to Harriet. What else could be expected when she is a self-declared "imaginist":

Could a linguist, could a grammarian, could even a mathematician have seen what she did, have witnessed their appearance together, and heard their history of it, without feeling that circumstances had been at work to make them peculiarly interesting to each other?—How much more must an imaginist, like herself, be on fire with speculation and foresight!— especially with such a ground-work of anticipation as her mind had already made. (335)

We meet no grammarians in *Emma*: but Mr Knightley opposes her imaginings as vigorously as her fancies. As conscious spokesman for his sex, he bluntly rejects the imaginings she attributes to them

(60). And, for his own part, he can scarcely tolerate the use of the mere word:

"Can you imagine any thing nearer perfect beauty than Emma altogether —face and figure?"
"I do not know what I could imagine, but I confess that I have seldom seen . . ." (39)

Accordingly, when he first notices "symptoms of intelligence" between Jane Fairfax and Frank Churchill, Mr Knightley tries to put them out of his mind, wishing to "escape any of Emma's errors of imagination" (343). Failing to do so, he afterwards reports his suspicions to Emma—and is roundly mocked:

"Oh! you amuse me excessively. I am delighted to find that you can vouchsafe to let your imagination wander—but it will not do—very sorry to check you in your first essay—but indeed it will not do. There is no admiration between them, I do assure you." (350)

The joke, of course, is really at the expense of Emma, an imaginist whose imagination has never yet led her to so subtle an insight.

But it is much more than a neat little joke. It is too soon to consider how Emma's over-confident declaration dismays Mr Knightley and affects his later actions. The immediate point is that Mr Knightley's imaginative insight into this affair makes one leading instance of a severance, in *Emma*, between "fancy" and "imagination". For "imagination" is sometimes applied to operations of the mind to which "fancy" only once attains; and, through this particular usage, *Emma* transcends the strict Johnsonian antithesis between "imagination" and "reason".

In the first place, "imagination" is used in neutral senses much more often than "fancy". Even though Emma laughs at John Knightley for "'imagining me to be Mr. Elton's object'", there is nothing laughable in his reply: "'Such an imagination has crossed me, I own, Emma; and if it never occurred to you before, you may as well take it into consideration now'" (112). The point is borne out in a later reflection of Emma's: "'Can it really be as my brother imagined?'" (118) Because of Mrs Churchill's seizure, Frank Churchill dares "not yet, even in his own imagination, fix a time for coming to Randalls again" (266). After Emma has agreed to marry Mr Knightley, her father is still "without the most distant imagination of the impending evil" (434). And, in admitting her guilt to Mrs Weston, Jane Fairfax is emphatic on one point: "'Do not imagine, madam,' she continued, 'that I was taught wrong. . . . The error has been all my own'" (419).

47

But it is necessary to go beyond these neutral instances. There are occasions, some of them minor (396, 443), on which "imagination" is seen as positively creditable. Even Emma herself, the vain imaginist can rise quite unsolicited to a sympathetic gesture. When Elton snubs Mrs Weston by refusing to dance with Harriet, "Emma could imagine with what surprise and mortification she must be returning to her seat" (327-8). When Emma learns of Jane Fairfax's engagement, she "could now imagine why her own attentions had been slighted. . . . In Jane's eyes she had been a rival" (403). And, similarly, there are at least three occasions when Emma's "imagination" (119, 122, 188) alone gives her a completely accurate insight into the Westons' hopes for her.

In taking stock of our findings, we may usefully return first to our point of departure. Whether or not she had her "dear Dr. Johnson" (*Letters*, p. 181) in mind, Jane Austen clearly makes extensive use of a Johnsonian antithesis between right reason and the airy notions of fancy and imagination, an antithesis which expresses, in one prominent aspect, the conflict between Mr Knightley and Emma respectively. If there were no other departures from this broad antithesis than those instances where Mr Knightley waxes pompous in his defence of reason and the one instance where Emma's fancy envisages Mr Knightley himself as an emblem of the masculine virtues, there would be no call for any larger conclusion than that Jane Austen uses words with the freedom of a novelist rather than the necessary rigidity of a lexicographer. But the antithesis is quite transcended in those passages where reason requires the support of affection and those others where imagination (but not fancy) leads Emma and Mr Knightley to insights not otherwise attainable. For Johnson, I believe, reason is a beleaguered garrison, assailed on all sides by the blind impulses of man's lower nature and betrayed from within by vain fancies and imaginings: but in *Emma* the opposing forces can hope for reconciliation and mutual enrichment.

Emma's imagination is at its best when Mrs Weston is its subject. Besides the examples already mentioned, there is a striking passage where—though the word "imagination" is not used—Emma achieves the same emotional *rapport*. Mrs Weston has asked Emma to spare her a thought on the day of her step-son's arrival:

. . . Mrs. Weston's faithful pupil did not forget either at ten, or eleven, or twelve o'clock, that she was to think of her at four.

"My dear, dear, anxious friend,"—said she, in mental soliloquy, while walking down stairs from her own room, "always over-careful for every body's comfort but your own; I see you now in all your little fidgets, going again and again into his room, to be sure that all is right." (189)

Such imaginings as these are very far from the heartless ingenuity that Emma exercises on her acquaintance at large. The essential difference is that Mrs Weston is not one of her puppets but a person whom she knows and loves. Reverting, then, to the point where this phase of our discussion began—that is, to Emma's resolution of "repressing imagination all the rest of her life" (142)—one must conclude that her resolution is not only futile but positively undesirable. What Emma really needs to do is to discover more of others and of herself: so enriched, her imagination will work as freely, but to more sympathetic ends.

V

The notion that Emma is long at fault not through being imaginative but through holding, in general, to an emotionally barren conception of imagination is borne out, paradoxically enough, by her indulgence in reasonings no less barren. On one such occasion, she treats of love and marriage with just that calculating rationalism which, if only for Professor Schorer, pervades the whole novel.[18] On the same terms as she had prescribed marriage for Harriet and Mr Elton (35), she now prescribes celibacy for herself. Even the fluent rhythms

---

18. Sir Walter Scott was the first to complain that 'calculating prudence' is allowed an undue influence on those who marry in Jane Austen's novels, as when Elizabeth Bennet is converted by seeing the 'very handsome seat and grounds belonging to her admirer' ('*Emma*', *Quarterly Review*, Vol. xiv (1815), p. 194). But, as A. C. Bradley implies, the example rests on a misreading of *Pride and Prejudice* ('Jane Austen', *Essays and Studies*, Vol. ii (1911), p. 31n.). And this same Elizabeth gives a sufficient answer to Scott's more general contention: "She had always felt that Charlotte's opinion of matrimony was not exactly like her own, but she could not have supposed it possible that when called into action, she would have sacrificed every better feeling to worldly advantage" (*Pride and Prejudice*, p. 125).

But Professor Schorer goes much further. His method is to assemble a large number of 'buried or dead metaphors' and to suggest that they spring to life from mutual propinquity. His list begins with 'all that metaphor of high and low, sink and rise, advance and decline, superior and inferior, rank and fortune, power and command; as "held below the level," "raise her expectations too high," "materially cast down," "the intimacy between her and Emma must sink." ' Such metaphors, he contends, 'imply one consistent set of values . . . the values of commerce and property . . . It would seem that we are in a world of peculiarly *material* value, a world of almost instinctive material interests in its basic, intuitive response to experience.' And he goes on to speak of the 'tension' between this submerged presence and the 'refined sensibility' that occupies the surface of *Emma* ('The Humiliation of Emma Woodhouse' in Ian Watt (ed.), *Jane Austen*, pp. 99-100). The central fallacies here are just those that were widely recognized in Dr Caroline Spurgeon's well-known collection of Shakespearian 'images'. Yet even the much-abused Dr Spurgeon took the precaution of comparing Shakespeare's images with those of other writers.

49

of her ordinary speech stiffen into the pattern of a logic exercise as
she neatly distinguishes various self-interested grounds for marrying
—and exempts herself from each:

> "I have none of the usual inducements of women to marry. Were I to
> fall in love, indeed, it would be a different thing! but I have never been in
> love; it is not my way, or my nature; and I do not think I ever shall. And,
> without love, I am sure I should be a fool to change such a situation as
> mine. Fortune I do not want; employment I do not want; consequence I
> do not want: I believe few married women are half as much mistress of
> their husband's house, as I am of Hartfield; and never, never could I
> expect to be so truly beloved and important; so always first and always
> right in any man's eyes as I am in my father's." (84)

Emma's glibness is certainly not tempered by the references to love
with which she begins and ends. To be "truly beloved", it seems, is
to be regarded as "always first and always right"; and Emma justly
assumes that she can no more count on finding a husband who will
unfailingly surrender to her than she herself could brook becoming
so docile a wife. Her error here lies not in her inferences but in her
premise. The love that grows between Elinor Dashwood and
Edward Ferrars, between Catherine Morland and Henry Tilney,
or, more powerfully, between Anne Elliot and Frederick Wentworth
is less absolute than Emma now requires. It is, indeed, more nearly
akin to the modest, mutual happiness which people generally can
hope to achieve and which Emma and Mr Knightley will themselves discover.

Having unwittingly prompted Emma's disquisition, Harriet has
many a "Dear me!" for so unconventional an answer. A perfect
repository of the conventional pieties, she now raises one more of
the usual inducements for marrying—the danger of becoming an
old maid, like Miss Bates. Emma attempts a rational answer but
merely betrays her underlying confusion. The thought of becoming
like Miss Bates is "'as formidable an image as [Harriet] could
present'" (84). But there is no occasion for that: "'it is poverty only
which makes celibacy contemptible to a generous public'" (85). In
the following sentences, Emma tacitly withdraws the stinging irony
of "generous" and accepts the public's very ground for distinguishing
between pleasant single women and disagreeable old maids. Now
the idea that "'a very narrow income has a tendency to contract
the mind, and sour the temper'" (85) is certainly not foolish. But,
as Emma's own account of Miss Bates immediately shows, poverty
alone cannot produce the whole difference between a pleasant and
a disagreeable person, married or single. Again, Emma's conviction
that she herself would make a contented spinster is belied by her

very natural discontent with Highbury and her father's little circle, by her history of flirting half-heartedly with just those pastimes on which she claims she will rely, and by the deep ennui reflected in her restless fancies. Her belief that the "'comfort'" of independent living would suit her better than "'what is warmer and blinder'" (86) is belied by her affectionate dependence upon her father and Mrs Weston. And her declared preference for nieces and nephews over children of her own is to be exploded by the affair of little Henry and Donwell Abbey. Like Emma the imaginist, in short, the rationalistic Emma takes too little account of the force of emotion in human intercourse.

These confusions cry out for more challenging opposition than Emma usually meets. If Harriet's habitual "Dear me!" expresses only an inane surprise, her "To be sure!" makes for a show of agreement no less servile than Elton's "Exactly so" and no less vacuous than the fearful quibblings of Mr Woodhouse. Nor can Emma's needs be met by Harriet's mindless capacity to slide from seriously intended remarks on nieces generally to gossip about Miss Bates' niece (86). But Emma's lack of a more challenging companion is only one manifestation among many of the narrowness of her circle. Apart from the Westons, whose love is far removed—in the narrator's striking phrase—from "the tyrannic influence of youth on youth" (16), the Knightleys are the only married couple of her close acquaintance. Their influence is shown when, in the chapter following her disquisition upon marriage, they are brought to Hartfield for a brief visit.

As an individual character, Isabella has little part to play. She commiserates, at due length, with her father on the loss of poor Miss Taylor. She shares his taste for gruel, his idea of conversation, and his imperfect understanding (95: cf. 13). And, while her preference in apothecaries must differ, her health is no less in her mind. Though father and daughter are at one in "a general benevolence of temper, and a strong habit of regard for every old acquaintance" (92), Isabella too often overtaxes her friends' desire to praise her children. Apart from these comic touches, she is the first of many who construe Frank Churchill in terms of their own preoccupations (96) and who irritate Emma by rehearsing Jane Fairfax's merits as a friend (104). After this one visit, however, Isabella's only service is from afar (451). The novel does not require a second Mr Woodhouse; and her chief purpose is quickly served.

For, whether in mere analogy or as an implied cause, Isabella's marriage sheds light on Emma's desire to remain single. John Knightley, undoubtedly, is "always first and always right" in the eyes of his wife, who considers him "'one of the very best tempered men that ever existed'" (95). During his worst fit of ill-temper, she declares her pity for the Churchills: "'To be constantly living with an ill-tempered person, must be dreadful. It is what we happily have never known any thing of; but it must be a life of misery'" (121). Only through such amiable blindness can Isabella remain "a model of right feminine happiness", "passing her life with those she doated on, full of their merits, blind to their faults, and always innocently busy" (140). For the temper she so admires is made the subject not merely of Emma's prejudice but also of the narrator's exact judgement:

He was not an ill-tempered man, not so often unreasonably cross as to deserve such a reproach; but his temper was not his great perfection; and, indeed, with such a worshipping wife, it was hardly possible that any natural defects in it should not be increased. The extreme sweetness of her temper must hurt his. He had all the clearness and quickness of mind which she wanted, and he could sometimes act an ungracious, or say a severe thing. He was not a great favourite with his fair sister-in-law. Nothing wrong in him escaped her (92-3).

During most of his present stay at Hartfield, his few caustic remarks are accepted, even by Emma, as fully justified. But his reputation is quite upheld when the whole party visits Randalls. He is so seriously annoyed by being taken from home on a wintry evening that Emma can only remind herself that, in remaining single, she need never defer to such a man.

Jane Austen is not content to make this one point, important as it is. In the cause of John Knightley's ill-humour on this occasion, a new and major area of interest first manifests itself; and, simultaneously, there is a marked broadening of the narrative. In the first ninety-odd pages of the novel, there is only one occasion (47-8) when more than two of three characters speak together. Each little group has made its separate bow; each individual among them has been examined through Emma's eyes; and, for each of them, the narrator has enabled us to see more than Emma's prejudices reveal. With all this established, Jane Austen is able to enter upon more complex scenes of social intercourse and so to enrich her argument and Emma's view of life. Everything still relates, of course, to Emma and Mr Knightley and, after each large phase of the action, the two of them are still brought face to face. But, from this time, there are long periods during which Mr Knightley hardly speaks, periods during which, for example, widely differing attitudes to social intercourse itself are subtly juxtaposed.

Thus John Knightley's display of ill-temper is caused by being obliged, to his mind pointlessly, to seek the company of his fellows.

His whole manner shows that this is no passing fit of spleen but the thoughtful, however intemperate, expression of a reasoned attitude of mind. He begins in the aphoristic fashion of his brother, marshals his argument just as his brother might do, and even catches his brother's Johnsonian note when he invokes "the voice of nature":

"A man," said he, "must have a very good opinion of himself when he asks people to leave their own fireside, and encounter such a day as this, for the sake of coming to see him. He must think himself a most agreeable fellow; I could not do such a thing. It is the greatest absurdity—Actually snowing at this moment!—The folly of not allowing people to be comfortable at home—and the folly of people's not staying comfortably at home when they can! If we were obliged to go out such an evening as this, by any call of duty or business, what a hardship we should deem it;—and here are we, probably with rather thinner clothing than usual, setting forward voluntarily, without excuse, in defiance of the voice of nature, which tells man, in every thing given to his view or his feelings, to stay at home himself, and keep all under shelter that he can;—here are we setting forward to spend five dull hours in another man's house, with nothing to say or to hear that was not said and heard yesterday, and may not be said and heard again to-morrow. Going in dismal weather, to return probably in worse;—four horses and four servants taken out for nothing but to convey five idle, shivering creatures into colder rooms and worse company than they might have had at home." (113)

Now, as we have seen, Emma is too busy congratulating herself on not being his wife to offer any reply. But, upon their reaching the vicarage, a reply of a sort announces itself. For Elton is full of the sociable chatter from which John Knightley quails. The weather is not so much cold as seasonable; the contrivances of modern days quite keep the cold at bay; they can be sure of excellent fires at Randalls; and, if they should be snowed up, there can be nothing but pleasure in the prospect of a week's stay. As he rattles on, he and John Knightley travel further and further beyond each other's comprehension—until John Knightley ends both journey and chapter by declaring roundly that "'My first enjoyment . . . will be to find myself safe at Hartfield again'" (116).

Now Elton has a special motive for so rejoicing in this visit, and we are reminded of it by his inflated manner towards Emma: "'I think you will agree with me, (turning with a soft air to Emma,) I think I shall certainly have your approbation. . .'" (116). There is a further reason why he cannot long serve as foil to John Knightley. After his rejection by Emma, later that evening, he will appear seldom and be given only three or four brief speeches in all the rest of the novel. His actively unpleasant qualities are to be supplied, with interest, by the charming Augusta. But his shallow sociability is to be the province of Mr Weston.

Although Elton and Weston are very different creatures, they are brought together, in this one important quality, by the novel itself. Weston's sociability has been emphasized whenever he has been mentioned. Elton confers a doubtful blessing on him by remarking that "'he is exactly what one values, so hospitable, and so fond of society'" (116). And Weston echoes Elton's wish that the whole party be snow-bound. Weston's friendly little confidences about his arch-enemy, Mrs Churchill, are not seen at their worst until he speaks openly to so recent an acquaintance as Mrs Elton (306-7). But his leanings are already betrayed by being set in contrast with the perfectly proper admissions of his wife.

After dinner that evening, when John Knightley dismays Mr Woodhouse with news of heavy snow outside and goes on "pursuing his triumph rather unfeelingly" (126), the same word is used again:

> Mr. Weston, with triumph of a different sort, was confessing that he had known it to be snowing some time, but had not said a word, lest it should make Mr. Woodhouse uncomfortable, and be an excuse for his hurrying away. As to there being any quantity of snow fallen or likely to fall to impede their return, that was a mere joke; he was afraid they would find no difficulty. He wished the road might be impassable, that he might be able to keep them all at Randalls. (126)

In their different ways, both Weston and John Knightley are inattentive to the real happiness of their friends here gathered and of Mr Woodhouse in particular. (Weston, moreover, ignores his wife's embarrassment at having to accommodate so large a party in two spare rooms.) The chief difference between them is that John Knightley afterwards has the grace to be "ashamed of his ill-humour" (133) and to behave with an "amiableness [that] never failed him during the rest of his stay at Hartfield" (139). Unconscious of any fault, Weston simply goes on being Weston.

In so far as her companions' behaviour relates to these broader issues, it glances off the surface of Emma's mind. Her earlier aspersions on Elton's "'passion for dining out'" (111), which might pass as a reflection on men of selfish sociability, are really no more than a puzzled attempt to explain his willingness to forsake Harriet. Though Weston displays just such a sociability, Emma does not notice it, and he long remains "a great favourite" (117) with her. Admittedly she discovers "something honourable and valuable in the strong domestic habits" of John Knightley and sees there the cause of his "disposition to look down on the common rate of social intercourse, and those to whom it was important" (97). Even this, however, is a reluctant concession the implications of which she does not seriously pursue until the evening of the ball at the Crown Inn.

And yet here, as so often, Emma's natural instincts are more judicious than her ideas. It is not merely for the sake of "eating and drinking, and playing whist with [her] neighbours" (96) that she goes to Randalls. Nor, on the other hand, is she deterred by the prospect of "five dull hours in another man's house" (113). She goes because "the very sight of Mrs. Weston, her smile, her touch, her voice was grateful to Emma" (117). In describing this relationship in such warm terms just when she is representing selfish aloofness and selfish sociability, Jane Austen is pointing not only to the existence of a middle way but also to Emma's latent ability to find that way. And if Emma's relationship with Mrs Weston is too special to shed a general light, that relationship does not stand alone. Ever since their quarrel about Robert Martin, only recently patched up, George Knightley has appeared seldom and spoken less. Each time he has appeared, however, he has shown a genuine social grace that animadverts strongly on the extremes represented by his brother and Weston. On the visitors' first evening at Hartfield, he joins with Emma in keeping the peace: while she steers her father away from dangerous topics, he distracts his brother from things that have already been said. And, on the evening at Randalls, while his brother and his host are celebrating their different triumphs, he quietly establishes that the party can safely get home and then joins with Emma in securing a prompt departure.

Why, then, does he figure so seldom in this part of the novel? In the two chapters about the party at Randalls, he utters only a dozen words. Perhaps he is silenced by the news of Frank Churchill's coming. But, since it is still about a fortnight before his jealousy is really aroused, it seems more likely that Jane Austen has another purpose. Clearly Mr Knightley is being set in contrast with his brother and Weston: yet, if the contrast were made too plain, even Emma could hardly miss the point. As it is, Emma can take his services for granted; and, when they are next shown together, they quarrel bitterly about Frank Churchill.

VI

This longest and most damaging of all their quarrels is ostensibly concerned with Frank Churchill's ability to visit Randalls. As when they quarrelled about Harriet's birth, they both defy their ignorance of the facts: but, now as then, the facts must make our starting-point. Clearly this particular visit need not have been postponed. Though Frank Churchill's letter of excuse expresses a "'very great mortification and regret'" (144), he subsequently admits that the "'visit might have been sooner paid'" and that he "'did not come till Miss Fairfax was in Highbury'" (437). The larger question of whether, in general, he might come if he chose cannot be answered so simply. The Westons' belief that visits to them are prevented by Enscombe's special interdict has no real foundation: he meets his father annually in London (17); and he does eventually visit Randalls. Re-phrasing the question, then, we must ask whether he is free to go visiting when he chooses—or is tied too closely to his aunt's purse-strings.[19] The clearest comment is his own: "though he had his separate engagements, it was not without difficulty, without considerable address *at times*, that he could get away, or introduce an acquaintance for a night" (221). This statement is borne out by his behaviour *after* Jane Fairfax comes to Highbury. He is certainly free to come "at times". Yet he is much distressed by the curtailment of his first visit, and uncertain whether he can return from Yorkshire. When the Churchills are staying in London, he is kept from Highbury for full ten days. And, even after they remove to Richmond, he is almost obliged to give up the party at Donwell Abbey.

The quarrel between Emma and Mr Knightley is prefigured by a milder dispute between Emma and Mrs Weston. Having no real grounds for an opinion on the matter, Mrs Weston relies on her husband and possibly also on her step-son's apologetic letters, in which he might well play Spenlow to Mrs Churchill's Jorkins. As she tells Emma, "'I cannot bear to imagine any reluctance on his side; but I am sure there is a great wish on the Churchills' to keep him to themselves'" (122). Emma replies with a flat assertion that "'He ought to come. . . . If he could stay only a couple of days, he ought to come; and one can hardly conceive a young man's not having it in his power to do as much as that'"(122). Against Emma's easy generalizations about filial duty in young men and her empty theorizings about "'my idea of Mrs. Churchill'" (123), Mrs Weston quietly but steadily adduces the force of circumstance in all human affairs and their own ignorance of Frank Churchill's particular circumstances at Enscombe. Enscombe is not to be judged by general rules, and he may have considerable influence at some times and on some points while yet finding it "'perfectly impossible . . . to know beforehand *when* it will be'" (123). But all this has no immediate effect: "Emma listened, and then coolly said, 'I shall not be satisfied, unless he comes'" (123).

In a novel of any moral subtlety, as in real life, dogmatism cannot

19. At no point does anyone, even Mr Knightley, insinuate that Frank Churchill is seeking dead men's shoes: all admit that he owes a dual allegiance; but some question whether he pays enough respect to his father's side of it.

simply be justified by the verdict of later events. Though Emma is proved right on this occasion, Mrs Weston's attitude remains the more congenial. And yet, if Emma judges Frank Churchill dogmatically, her motives are not ungenerous. Although she has a "great curiosity to see him" (119) for herself, she is still more keenly aware of all that the visit means to the step-mother, torn between hope and fear: "'And so you do not consider this visit from your son as by any means certain. I am sorry for it. The introduction must be unpleasant, whenever it takes place; and the sooner it could be over, the better'" (122). Again, Emma's refusal to discuss the matter except with her real intimates must stand to her credit. She knows that "Mrs. Weston would speak to her, with a degree of unreserve which she would not hazard with Isabella" (122); and she, likewise, politely rebuffs John Knightley by keeping to the simple facts (95).

There are obvious technical advantages in having Frank Churchill's visit canvassed before the Elton fiasco and Elton's ensuing disappearance from the scene. And there are pleasing ironies in seeing Emma induced first to rebuff John Knightley's implicit disapproval of Frank Churchill's delay, then to express her own disapproval to Mrs Weston, and finally to defend the young man against the stern disapproval of Mr Knightley. But Jane Austen's capacity for bringing different events into significant relationships goes deeper than that. Because Emma's quarrel with Mr Knightley has its roots in the Elton affair, the resulting breach between them becomes her worst punishment yet for interfering in others' lives. Deeply impressed by Harriet's demeanour on being told of Mr Elton's true intention, Emma goes home, as we have seen, "with every previous resolution confirmed of being humble and discreet, and repressing imagination all the rest of her life" (142). In this mood, she hears of Frank Churchill's letter of excuse and is obliged, not only for the Westons' sake but also because she must conceal every trace of the contretemps with Elton, to affect more interest and more disappointment than she feels. No harm is done at Randalls. But when she tells the news to Mr Knightley—exclaiming "quite as much as was necessary, (or, being acting a part, perhaps rather more,) at the conduct of the Churchills, in keeping him away" (145) —his response amuses, astonishes, and at last dismays her.

Mr Knightley begins by declaring that, while "'the Churchills are very likely in fault'", Frank Churchill certainly "'might come if he would'" (145). He has no doubt "'learnt to be above his connections'" (145). A man of his age could hardly be confined to Enscombe. His duty is to visit Randalls; his letters prove he knows it; and his tardiness can only be construed as neglect.

In essence it is an impressive case. But it is injured, from the very first, by Mr Knightley's stooping repeatedly to cheaper tactics than he need. On no better evidence than a visit to Weymouth, he asserts that Frank Churchill has so much money and leisure "'that he is glad to get rid of them at the idlest haunts in the kingdom. We hear of him for ever at some watering-place or other'" (146). Again, he tampers with Frank Churchill's age as best suits his immediate purpose. We know that he is twenty-three (96). When it suits Mr Knightley to hold him fully responsible for his actions, he twice makes him "'three or four-and-twenty'" (145-6), only to restore him to "'three-and-twenty'" (150) when the argument is best served by treating him as a mere whipper-snapper. When Emma suggests that he may be able to leave Enscombe "at times", Mr Knightley has no grounds but prejudice for retorting that "'those times are, whenever he thinks it worth his while; whenever there is any temptation of pleasure'" (146). And, finally, there is something remorseless in the ease with which Mr Knightley moves, again and again, from generalizations about what "a man" should do to pat conclusions about what this particular young man can do, no matter what his circumstances.

"To her great amusement," we are told, Emma "perceived that she was taking the other side of the question from her real opinion, and making use of Mrs. Weston's arguments against herself" (145). This suggests, of course, that Emma is arguing only for the perverse pleasure she so often finds in opposing Mr Knightley. Even if she could forget her own earlier conviction that Frank Churchill "ought to come", she could not convincingly repudiate Mr Knightley's argument from filial duty. She is not the person to quibble over details like watering-places and Frank Churchill's age. The most promising line of attack, therefore, is Mrs Weston's emphasis on circumstance, her insistence on "at times".

As Emma follows that line, however, there is a gradual alteration in her tone, a growing sense that, by drawing analogies between his life and her own, she begins to appreciate Frank Churchill's difficulties. When she tells Mr Knightley, "'You do not know what it is to have tempers to manage'" (146), she speaks with the authority of recent painful experience. Had not Isabella, with Mrs Churchill's notorious ill-temper in mind, drawn a blissful contrast between the Enscombe family and her own, never dreaming that others, especially Emma, would find the case more apt for a comparison? Then, again, Emma says that "'Nobody, who has not been in the interior of a family, can say what the difficulties of any individual of that family may be'" (146). While she speaks with a discreet generality, she makes this point so much more sharply than Mrs Weston had done (123) that, sensing a real strength of feeling, one recalls an earlier allusion to her father's dampening influence: "'I think you must know Hartfield enough to comprehend that'" (13).

By virtue of this growing empathy with Frank Churchill, Emma has much the better of the clash between high principles and psychological realities that makes up the next phase of the argument. Mr Knightley asserts that "'a man who felt rightly'" would tell Mrs Churchill that he must visit his father: "'If he would say so to her at once, in the tone of decision becoming a man, there would be no opposition made to his going'" (146). With all the merciless brilliance of a younger Jane Austen, Emma replies that "'there might be some made to his coming back again'"; twice refers to Mr Knightley's want of imagination in supposing such conduct practicable; and pictures Frank Churchill "'standing up in the middle of the room, I suppose, and speaking as loud as he could!'" (147).

Where lesser men might quail, Mr Knightley stands unshaken. Certainly he cannot match the vivid power of Emma's little picture. But there is nothing to suggest that he is dissatisfied with the orotund generalities of his reply: the declaration would be "'made, of course, as a man of sense would make it, in a proper manner'"; "'a sensible man would find no difficulty in it'"(147). Having thus resolved any small practical difficulty, our sensible man rises to an almost Socratic conviction that they who know the Good will not forsake it. But, alas, he finds the gadfly of psychological reality about his ears once more:

"Respect for right conduct is felt by every body. If he would act in this sort of manner, on principle, consistently, regularly, their little minds would bend to his."

"I rather doubt that. You are very fond of bending little minds; but where little minds belong to rich people in authority, I think they have a knack of swelling out, till they are quite as unmanageable as great ones."
(147)

Emma then justly points out that he is thinking only of what he, as he now is, might do at Enscombe and forgetting that he "'would have no habits of early obedience and long observance to break through'" (147-8). But when she adds, incautiously, that Frank Churchill "'may have as strong a sense of what would be right, as you can have, without being so equal under particular circumstances to act up to it'", Mr Knightley argues as sturdily for victory as even Johnson could: "'Then [he retorts], it would not be so strong a sense. If it failed to produce equal exertion, it could not be an equal conviction'" (148). Encouraged, no doubt, by this vigorous sophistry, Mr Knightley discovers a more hopeful line of argument. Frank Churchill should not now, for the first time, be resisting an unjust claim: "'It ought to have been an habit with him by this time, of following his duty, instead of consulting expediency'" (148). Emma, in her turn, is put on the defensive and, after appealing to Mr Weston's high opinion of his son, can only add that a man need not be the worse for having a "'more yielding, complying, mild disposition than would suit your notions of man's perfection'" (148).

Following up his advantage, Mr Knightley turns from principles and speculations to the more concrete evidence of Frank Churchill's letters. Though he has no right, as yet, to speak of "'falsehoods'" (149), his own observation justifies his belief that such "'fine flourishing'" (148) letters "'do not satisfy Mrs. Weston. They hardly can satisfy a woman of her good sense and quick feelings'" (149). Mr Knightley clinches his case by reminding Emma that, because of Mrs Weston's social position, "'attention to Randalls is doubly due, and she must doubly feel the omission'" (149). But, even now, he cannot resist suggesting that, "'Had she been a person of consequence herself, he would have come I dare say'" (149). And, when Emma resorts to the desperate *ad hominem* of "'You seem determined to think ill of him'" (149), his very indignation bears out her charge.

The real argument is over but a few shafts remain. When Emma tactlessly pictures how Highbury will welcome Frank Churchill, "'what a *sensation*[20] his coming will produce'" (149), Mr Knightley asks her to "'excuse my being so much overpowered'" (150). Undeterred, she goes on to suggest that:

"My idea of him is, that he can adapt his conversation to the taste of every body, and has the power as well as the wish of being universally agreeable. To you, he will talk of farming; to me, of drawing or music; and so on to every body, having that general information on all subjects which will enable him to follow the lead, or take the lead, just as propriety may require, and to speak extremely well on each; . . ." (150)

20. Evidently *"sensation"* is italicized as a conscious vogue-word, used in the manner of Fanny Burney and marking Emma's airy way of picturing her unknown hero. This reading is confirmed by the absence of 'sensation' (in this sense) from Johnson's *Dictionary* and by a sentence of Southey's, written in 1818 and quoted in *The Oxford English Dictionary* (*see* 'sensation', 3b): 'His death produced what in the phraseology of the present day is called, a great sensation.'

"Introduction" (275) and *"mediocre"* (276) both relate to the modish affectations of Mrs Elton; both are missing, in the relevant senses, from Johnson; and, in both cases, Jane Austen herself is among the authorities cited in *The Oxford English Dictionary*. With *"recollecting"* (270), however, where the context suggests that the italics are for simple emphasis, the dictionaries cite relevant examples going back for several centuries.

This is scarcely an unreasonable "idea" (even though it is to be realized more thoroughly than Emma might wish); but Mr Knightley will have none of it and, as he twists her words against her, his prejudice appears more blatantly than ever:

"And mine," said Mr. Knightley warmly, "is, that if he turn out any thing like it, he will be the most insufferable fellow breathing! What! at three-and-twenty to be the king of his company—the great man—the practised politician, who is to read every body's character, and make every body's talents conduce to the display of his own superiority; ..." (150)

And he goes on, finally, to declare his complete uninterest in Frank Churchill, "with a degree of vexation, which made Emma immediately talk of something else, though she could not comprehend why he should be angry" (150).

If this whole quarrel is regarded as a debate on filial duty, albeit a heated one, honours are fairly even. In their ignorance of Frank Churchill's actual situation, as in their acceptance of his dual allegiance, there is little between them. In point of the argumentative proprieties, Emma is clearly the more scrupulous. In point of the verdict of events, Mr Knightley is proved right about this particular postponement but Emma is right in thinking that Frank Churchill's difficulties are virtually insuperable "at times". And, when events bring in this verdict, Emma, while having the more to concede, concedes it the more willingly. Mr Knightley admits that he was "'not quite impartial in my judgment'" (445). But, besides initiating the subject by reminding him that he was "'perfectly right'" (445), Emma makes no attempt to excuse herself, whether by appealing to those occasions when Frank Churchill *was* prevented from coming or by trying to tell him that her "real opinion" had originally coincided with his own.

But essentially the chapter is no more a debate than a case of measuring Emma against an absolute moral standard incarnate in Mr Knightley. Even those critics who acknowledge Mr Knightley's jealousy but regard it as a realistic wart on a character who might otherwise seem too flawless to be human have usually neglected the *dramatic* implications of this important incident. Professor Booth, for example, is more aware than many others that Mr Knightley 'lapses from perfection when he tries to judge Frank Churchill'.[21] But even Professor Booth can remark, in a more general context, that 'Jane Austen goes relatively deep morally, but scarcely skims the surface psychologically'.[22]

21. Wayne C. Booth, *The Rhetoric of Fiction*, p. 263.
22. Ibid., p. 163.

Such a judgement is the natural consequence of reducing a dramatic situation to a bare system of 'ideas'. In its rich apprehension of the interaction of circumstance and principle, the quarrel about Frank Churchill has 'moral depth' enough. But moral depth makes no account of dramatic considerations—no account, for example, of the fact that, a fortnight earlier, Emma herself was arguing for Frank Churchill's filial duty and over-riding Mrs Weston's protests about his circumstances. We have seen how Harriet's behaviour about Elton, her own shamefaced bravado, and Mr Knightley's asperity set off this remarkable change in Emma's attitude. Distracted, perhaps, by an undue attachment to *moral* depth, by the delusory ease of treating such a quarrel as if it were a debate from *Crotchet Castle*, or even by their faith in Mr Knightley's authorial function, those who have discussed *Emma* have overlooked a phenomenon which—whether dramatically or psychologically—seems to cut quite deep.

Nor is it an isolated phenomenon. We have seen how, quite unwittingly, Mr Knightley induces Emma to think of Frank Churchill more sympathetically (in the strict sense) than ever before. From now on, she will await his coming and treat his arrival with a more serious interest than appears in her earlier fancies about their being well suited to each other. And some of Emma's sallies, in turn, affront Mr Knightley more gravely than she knows. When she suggests that Frank Churchill may have a milder disposition than Mr Knightley would admire, she adds, "'though it may cut him off from some advantages, it will secure him many others'" (148). Whatever *her* meaning, only one such increase of advantage would occur to Mr Knightley. After tactlessly declaring herself much prejudiced in Frank Churchill's favour, she attributes this feeling to her love for the Westons (150): but her explanation comes too late. And, when Mr Knightley angrily exclaims that he hears of no other merits in Frank Churchill than "'that he is well grown and good-looking, with smooth, plausible manners'" (149), Emma, like Mrs Weston before her (41), forgets that Mr Knightley might think of himself as a young man and replies, "'Well, if he have nothing else to recommend him, he will be a treasure at Highbury. We do not often look upon fine young men, well-bred and agreeable. We must not be nice and ask for all the virtues into the bargain'" (149).

The whole quarrel, then, is less interesting as an illustration of Jane Austen's supposed ideas than as a dramatic climax worthy of this first volume. By the end of the chapter, only Jane Fairfax's presence is needed to make all ready for the entry of Frank Churchill. And, after entering this chapter on better terms than they have been for many weeks, Emma and Mr Knightley part more bitterly than ever. He retires to cure his wounds and nurse his jealousy. Apart from a lesser disagreement with Emma, about Jane Fairfax, he is scarcely seen for a hundred pages; and, in those moments when he does speak, it is to refuse to join a party of which Frank Churchill is a member or to pass some dour comment on a haircut, a musical duet, or the tediousness of dancing for all but the participants. For her part, Emma is left puzzled by what seems a groundless prejudice and dismayed by his anger. And, as she reflects on these departures from his usual habits of mind, we are enabled—as he has never been —to see how highly she esteems him:

To take a dislike to a young man, only because he appeared to be of a different disposition from himself, was unworthy the real liberality of mind which she was always used to acknowledge in him; for with all the high opinion of himself, which she had often laid to his charge, she had never before for a moment supposed it could make him unjust to the merit of another. (150-1)

CHAPTER II

Volume Two

I *M* *B*

As soon as the second volume of *Emma* begins, Jane Austen sets about enlarging her cast. She turns at once to the Bateses and Jane Fairfax, and delays Frank Churchill's arrival only long enough to conceal his true object not only from the keen ears and idle minds of Highbury but also from the reader. As has often been remarked, the chapters concerning Elton's engagement and the reappearance of Robert Martin are used to occupy—or, indeed, create—this period of delay. But such a delay does not, of itself, solve the whole problem. Certain facts, which can no longer be omitted, must somehow be played down. The implied connection between the meeting at Weymouth in late September and Jane Fairfax's troubled state during the autumn and winter is a case in point—a case in which Jane Austen's discreet shifts of narrative stance are of the utmost service. Part of the history of these months is recounted, for example, by the narrator speaking for the Campbells. Since they have no reason to connect Jane's decline with their visit to Weymouth and since their daughter's marriage did follow hard upon that visit, they leap to a conclusion so natural that it looks like the whole truth: Jane "had never been quite well since *the time of* their daughter's marriage" (165: my italics). As far as possible, Jane Fairfax herself is steered away from such dangerous topics; and, when this cannot be, she, too, is kept from telling the whole truth. The narrator, speaking for her, points out, for example, that she has lately reached the age at which "she had long resolved" (165) she should turn governess. She *had* made that resolution; she *has* now reached that age: nothing is omitted but those recent events which have altered all her hopes. And even the impersonal narrator's summing-up is as disingenuous as it is frank: "with regard to her not accompanying them to Ireland, her account to her aunt contained nothing but truth, though there might be some truths not told" (166). One cannot conceive of a reader so perceptive as to distinguish, at first sight, the true pattern in such gossamer. Yet all the threads are there.

Even in so delicate a phase of the novel, most subjects can be treated more simply than this one concealed relationship. The volume opens with Emma still serving out the self-imposed penance that obliges her to listen, kindly and patiently, while Harriet brings every conversation back to the inevitable Elton. Since she is still Emma, her capacity for punishment is not unlimited; and, on this particular morning, she eventually decides that a call upon the Bateses will at least supply a fresh variety of boredom.

Critics of *Emma* are more than usually in accord on the subject of Miss Bates. What might have become a contentious issue was raised by Sir Walter Scott, who suggested that, when 'characters of folly or simplicity' like 'old Woodhouse and Miss Bates' are 'too long dwelt upon, their prosing is apt to become as tiresome in fiction as in real society'.[1] But Archbishop Whately soon answered this contention so effectively that it has scarcely been revived: 'those who look with pleasure at Wilkie's pictures, or those of the Dutch school, must admit that excellence of imitation may confer attraction on that which would be insipid or disagreeable in the reality'.[2]

For a hundred years thereafter, critics were content to refer briefly to Miss Bates as a minor success in Jane Austen's comic vein; and it was left to Miss Lascelles to carry the matter further. Through the 'limpid confusion'[3] of Miss Bates' unique idiom, we are given information not otherwise available and encouraged to draw inferences that might otherwise escape us. Miss Lascelles shows what lies within one or two of Miss Bates' monologues; and, given this example, more recent critics have dealt exhaustively with nearly every speech she makes. It is enough for us, therefore, simply to admit Miss Bates' narrative function and to take advantage of it as occasion may require.

Miss Bates is also made the focal point of moral questions of some delicacy. When she is first described, the narrator records how her "contented and grateful spirit" (21) rises above the narrowness and impoverishment of her situation. And, if she has little enough *cause* for satisfaction in the present, her future is bleak indeed. Yet, though the pathos of her situation must never be forgotten, it is only part of the truth: despite the sentimental cant of certain modern critics, Miss Bates is also presented, no less emphatically, as a very tedious woman. The impersonal narrator may well speak of "a pretty long speech from Miss Bates, which few persons listened to" (344). Only

---

1. [Walter Scott], '*Emma*', *Quarterly Review*, Vol. xiv (1815), p. 200.
2. [Richard Whately], 'Modern Novels', *Quarterly Review*, Vol. xxiv (1821), p. 362. The analogy of 'the Dutch school' appears regularly in early Austen criticism.
3. Mary Lascelles, *Jane Austen and Her Art*, p. 94.

Mr Woodhouse, to whom she is "exactly suited" (21), stands out against a consensus that includes the kindliest of her neighbours. Even the humble Perry makes bold to declare that she is "not the best companion for an invalid of that [i.e., a nervous] description" (389). Mrs Cole, it appears, quails inwardly when she discovers that she is to hear, rather more than twice over, a letter from Jane Fairfax. Mrs Weston says that Miss Bates "'is a good creature, but, as a constant companion, must be very tiresome'" (286). Jane Fairfax tries in vain to prevent one empty repetition among many (245). Not being subject to the strict restraint expected of a lady, Mr Knightley copes more easily with her endless chatter and so objects to it the less. As Mrs Weston says, he can always "'talk louder, and drown her voice'" (226). It seems an improbable suggestion: but, on the following morning, he achieves that very feat.

With one conspicuous exception, the Hartfield circle are able to accommodate themselves to their Miss Bates. Both Mr Woodhouse and Mr Knightley do what they can to ease the Bates' poverty; and, if the one is comfortably blind to poor Hetty's eccentricities, the other contrives to close his eyes. Frank Churchill declares that Miss Bates is "'a woman that one may, that one *must* laugh at; but that one would not wish to slight'" (260). And Mrs Weston remains kindly and courteous without giving up her private opinion or her sense of humour:

"How would he bear [asks Emma] to have Miss Bates belonging to him? —To have her haunting the Abbey, and thanking him all day long for his great kindness in marrying Jane?—'So very kind and obliging!—But he always had been such a very kind neighbour!' And then fly off, through half a sentence, to her mother's old petticoat. 'Not that it was such a very old petticoat either—for still it would last a great while—and, indeed, she must thankfully say that their petticoats were all very strong.'"

"For shame, Emma! Do not mimic her. You divert me against my conscience." (225)

Brilliant as it is, Emma's parody is less lightly intended than it may seem. Without really knowing why, Emma finds herself violently opposed to the very idea that Jane Fairfax may become Mrs Knightley; and she seizes on Miss Bates as one means, among others, of laughing it out of court. By the same token, Emma's description of Miss Bates as "'so silly—so satisfied—so smiling—so prosing—so undistinguishing and unfastidious—and so apt to tell every thing relative to every body'" (85) is a heated rejoinder to Harriet's inane suggestion that, simply by not marrying, Emma herself must become "'an old maid at last, like Miss Bates'" (84). And, as we shall see, even her notorious outburst at Box Hill reflects special influences at work on her that morning. All such immediate provocations apart, Emma remains conspicuous in her intolerance of Miss Bateses.

To approach Emma's underlying motives, which are even less accessible than usual, we must take account of the passages already quoted; of the assertion that Miss Bates "'is only too good natured and too silly to suit me'" (85); and of the long reflection that precedes Emma's first chronicled visit to the Bateses:

> Mrs. and Miss Bates loved to be called on, and she knew she was considered by the very few who presumed ever to see imperfection in her, as rather negligent in that respect, and as not contributing what she ought to the stock of their scanty comforts.
> She had had many a hint from Mr. Knightley and some from her own heart, as to her deficiency—but none were equal to counteract the persuasion of its being very disagreeable,—a waste of time—tiresome women—and all the horror of being in danger of falling in with the second rate and third rate of Highbury, who were calling on them for ever, and therefore she seldom went near them. (155)

The most obvious quality in all this medley of motives is precisely that it *is* a medley. Evidently Emma is trying to justify, especially to herself, an antipathy whose origin she does not understand. In the narrow and tedious Highbury round, of which she so often complains, she cannot fairly object to any "waste of time". The loving daughter of Mr Woodhouse, friend of Mr Weston, and voluntary patroness of Harriet Smith, can scarcely dislike empty chatter for its own sake. (Surely *Emma* is conspicuous among great novels for the narrow, local range of topics on which its characters converse?) And Emma's 'snobbish' response to Miss Bates' lowly acquaintances is too extravagant ("all the horror of being in danger") to be taken seriously. Since Emma's own account of her motives is inadequate, we must seek a little further.

The beginning of an answer is to be found in the complaint to which Emma most persistently recurs: Miss Bates is more contented and more grateful than she has any business to be. This astonishing complaint cannot have any other meaning than that, through imagining herself in Miss Bates' situation, Emma knows how ill *she* would endure it. It is just the note of an emotional adolescent, of a person sensitive enough to feel her neighbour's misfortune keenly yet unable to accept that she cannot really alter it. (Her treatment of Harriet Smith affords a pretty contrast: there—so she assumes—a stroke of her imagination can prepare Cinderella for Prince Charming; but Miss Bates' situation is very plainly beyond the powers of a would-be fairy godmother.) Whereas her father and

Mr Knightley try to help the Bateses while recognizing that "'it is so little one can venture to do'" (172), Emma lets frustration express itself in scorn whenever she is obliged to remember the difference between their life and hers. On the safe ground of Hartfield, Emma can treat them as if there were no gulf of fortune between them— and these efforts are unexpectedly rewarded by Mr Knightley's praise. So far as possible, however, she avoids their dark and narrow staircase. And she would rather give them no help at all than have every crumb from the Hartfield table made the subject of Miss Bates' "dreadful gratitude" (380).

Emma's gift of a hind-quarter of pork, in token of Jane Fairfax's arrival, is an exception whose outcome is well calculated to confirm her in her rule. For Miss Bates comes rushing in, "full of thanks, and full of news":

"Oh! my dear sir, how are you this morning? My dear Miss Woodhouse —I come quite overpowered. Such a beautiful hind-quarter of pork! You are too bountiful! Have you heard the news? Mr. Elton is going to be married.". . .

"My dear sir, you really are too bountiful. My mother desires her very best compliments and regards, and a thousand thanks, and says you really quite oppress her.". . .

"Oh! my dear sir, as my mother says, our friends are only too good to us. If ever there were people who, without having great wealth themselves, had every thing they could wish for, I am sure it is us. We may well say that 'our lot is cast in a goodly heritage.' " (172-4)

One would naturally wish to clinch one's hypothesis by showing Emma shrinking back and privately disavowing the impulse that had led her to make the gift. But the moment is lost: Emma's attention is given entirely to the news of Mr Elton and—alas for her concealments!—to Mr Knightley's knowing smile. And, by the time she permits herself to make the Bateses another gift, she is a very different Emma. Under these conditions, the best corroboration available lies in the 'new' Emma's treatment of the Bateses. In the matter of visits, she calls on Miss Bates in quite an altered spirit (377ff.). And, in the matter of gifts, she has learnt to regard even small gestures as of value and to regard the needs of the recipient as surpassing the possible embarrassment of the donor: not even Miss Bates' gratitude is allowed to stand in the way of Emma's attempts to find something, however trifling, that will give comfort to Jane Fairfax (390-1).

Yet Jane Austen does not permit herself, even at this stage, to slur over the inextinguishable tediousness of Miss Bates. The torrent of words still rushes on while Emma quietly turns her mind to other things: "There was nothing in all this either to astonish or interest"

(384). Nor is Emma's contrition sentimentalized into an inhuman perfection. On this occasion, as on others, Emma would have done well to sift wheat from chaff. For Miss Bates is unwittingly revealing that Jane Fairfax's recent actions are deeply influenced by Frank Churchill's. We are, in short, shown enough of the new Emma to believe in her contrition and to see that her fierce intolerance has given way to just such a decent honesty as Mrs Weston's. We are not asked to accept that either she or Miss Bates is miraculously transformed.

II

Apart from its intrinsic importance, Emma's original attitude to Miss Bates has far-reaching side-effects. For her fantasy about Jane Fairfax and Mr Dixon originates in her belief that, like herself, Jane Fairfax must find Miss Bates' company uncongenial and her life one of privation. Certainly Emma's particular choice of a protagonist for her fantasy has more grounds than one: her mind is only too easily animated by the tale of the rescue at Weymouth, by the thought of Miss Fairfax's "decided superiority both in beauty and acquirements" (165) over Miss Campbell, and by the suggestions of a romantic 'decline' from the time of the Dixons' wedding. But Emma's need to devise this fantasy at all originates in her astonishment that, "'in spite of all her friend's urgency, and her own wish of seeing Ireland, Miss Fairfax prefers devoting the time to you and Mrs. Bates'" (161). She will put the same thought more plainly to Frank Churchill:

" . . . there must be a particular cause for her chusing to come to Highbury instead of going with the Campbells to Ireland. Here, she must be leading a life of privation and penance; there it would have been all enjoyment. As to the pretence of trying her native air, I look upon that as a mere excuse.—In the summer it might have passed; but what can any body's native air do for them in the months of January, February, and March?" (217)

Save for the legend of Harriet's gentle birth, the matter of Dixon is the most enduring of Emma's fancies. It takes account of most of the available evidence, including some that a less shrewd observer would have missed. And it is flexible enough to be varied as appearances alter: an air of quiet acceptance of a barren future can suggest a "simple, single, successless love on her side alone" (168); a "deep blush of consciousness" and "a smile of secret delight" can suggest more "reprehensible feelings" (243). After all, Emma is working on appropriate lines: her error lies in paying so much attention to the young man who went from Weymouth to Ireland that she overlooks the young man who has come from Weymouth to Highbury.

And yet the Dixon fantasy could never have begun if Emma and Jane Fairfax had become close friends. The most striking thing about Emma's feeling of dislike is that it has less to do with Jane Fairfax herself than with the influence of others. After their first meeting of Jane Fairfax's present visit, Emma admits to herself that "it was a dislike so little just—every imputed fault was so magnified by fancy, that she never saw Jane Fairfax the first time after any considerable absence, without feeling that she had injured her" (167). With a little flurry of "elegants" and a lament that she can think of no suitable husband, Emma resolves to treat her differently in future. Although this resolution is soon overcome by a revived dislike, it is not merely because "'Miss Fairfax is reserved'" (171). There is the inevitable aunt, who was tiresome enough when her niece's letters were her ammunition but grows more tiresome still when Jane Fairfax is there in person: "anxiety for her health was now added to admiration of her powers; and they had to listen to the description of exactly how little bread and butter she ate for breakfast . . ." (168). And Isabella is only one among those who so insist that dear Emma and the delightful Jane were born to be friends that a much less perverse creature than Emma would flee in dismay.

But Emma's strongest motive for dislike is her sense that Jane Fairfax is her rival. When she finally repents her "past injustice towards Miss Fairfax", she blushes for "the envious feelings which had certainly been, in some measure, the cause" (421). It is usual to overlook the "in some measure" and to suggest, besides, that Emma's envy is simply for the accomplishments of one who, unlike herself, has profited from the opportunities of her youth. The evidence usually adduced concerns Emma's inferior powers as a musician and her plans, forever postponed, of reading more seriously.

And yet, at least in this conventional form, the notion of envy does not really accord with the facts. We are told that Emma resigned her place at the pianoforte to Miss Fairfax, "whose performance, both vocal and instrumental, she never could attempt to conceal from herself, was infinitely superior to her own" (227). We are also told that she "did unfeignedly and unequivocally regret" this state of affairs and "most heartily grieve over the idleness of her childhood" (231): but, besides being directed entirely at herself, these strictures lead only to a little vigorous practice. Again, when she could easily accept the worthless compliments of Harriet, Emma persists with the truth: "'My playing is no more like her's, than a lamp is like sunshine. . . . Those who knew any thing about it, must have felt the difference'" (231-2). She will not even allow the time-honoured evasion—passed on by Harriet from Frank Churchill—of putting "taste" before "execution": "'Ah! but Jane Fairfax has them both, Harriet'" (232). Emma's one moment of bitterness occurs, most excusably, when she fears that Jane Fairfax means to patronize her (169). Once this moment is past, Emma remains willing honestly to admit her own inferior powers, justly to blame her own idleness, and yet naturally to prefer pastimes like dancing, "in which she need not blush to compare herself with Jane Fairfax" (247).

All this is far from the language of envy; and Jane Fairfax's accomplishments arouse Emma's dislike only because Mr Knightley admires them as he does:

Why she did not like Jane Fairfax might be a difficult question to answer; Mr. Knightley had once told her it was because she saw in her the really accomplished young woman, which she wanted to be thought herself; and though the accusation had been eagerly refuted at the time, there were moments of self-examination in which her conscience could not quite acquit her. (166)

Although Emma is more concerned by his admonishing her through such a comparison than by the admonition itself, we must not expect so potent a distinction to be stated openly at this stage of events. On the face of it, we are offered no more than Emma's habitual response to his recriminations, beginning in an eager rebuttal and ending in a troubled mood of introspection. Our real evidence lies rather in actions and reactions. Thus the underlying link between Emma's recognition that Mr Knightley approves highly of Jane Fairfax, his willingness to hold her up as a shining example, and Emma's dislike for her begins to emerge when (inspired by the mystery of the piano) Mrs Weston suggests that Mr Knightley may be thinking of Miss Fairfax as the prospective mistress of Donwell Abbey. Emma leaps instantly to the defence of little Henry Knightley, heir apparent to the Donwell estate, and declares, besides, that "'every feeling revolts'" (225). Yet, for all her swift denials, Emma's confidence is badly shaken.

When Mr Knightley joins them soon afterwards, Emma begins looking for "a sort of touchstone" (228). Since his praise for Jane Fairfax's music and his reluctance to be praised for having made his carriage available seem natural and unconstrained, Emma is encouraged to "proceed another step" (228). She remarks the Campbells' generosity in giving the piano and, when Mr Knightley agrees "without the smallest apparent embarrassment" and adds

71

that "'Surprizes are foolish things'", "Emma could have taken her oath that Mr. Knightley had had no concern in giving the instrument" (228). Yet, the piano apart, he may not be "entirely free from peculiar attachment" (228). Emma is troubled, therefore, by his annoyance that Jane Fairfax should be allowed to sing herself hoarse, but then finds comfort in his not dancing:

This would be a trial. He was no dancer in general. If he were to be very alert in engaging Jane Fairfax now, it might augur something. There was no immediate appearance. No; he was talking to Mrs. Cole—he was looking on unconcerned; Jane was asked by somebody else, and he was still talking to Mrs. Cole. (229-30)

In the weeks that follow, Emma's doubts recur. There is, for example, the question of the proposed ball. Unaware that Mr Knightley's hostility to the idea is founded on jealousy of Frank Churchill, Emma finds her own jealousy once more assuaged: "It was not in compliment to Jane Fairfax however that he was so indifferent, or so indignant; he was not guided by *her* feelings in reprobating the ball, for *she* enjoyed the thought of it to an extraordinary degree" (258). But the appetite for reassurance grows by what it feeds on, and Emma's eventual requirement is for an unequivocal proof. Even now, one must emphasize, she misconstrues her own doubts: the cause of little Henry will only be forsaken when, knowing herself to be the prospective mistress of Donwell, she finds "amusement in detecting the real cause of that violent dislike of Mr. Knightley's marrying Jane Fairfax, or any body else, which at the time she had wholly imputed to the amiable solicitude of the sister and the aunt" (449-50). Little Henry's interests, then, are still uppermost when she puts Mr Knightley to the decisive test:

"I know how highly you think of Jane Fairfax," said Emma. Little Henry was in her thoughts, and a mixture of alarm and delicacy made her irresolute what else to say.

"Yes," he replied, "any body may know how highly I think of her."

"And yet," said Emma, beginning hastily and with an arch look, but soon stopping—it was better, however, to know the worst at once—she hurried on—"And yet, perhaps, you may hardly be aware yourself how highly it is. The extent of your admiration may take you by surprize some day or other." (287)

Mr Knightley needs only a few firm sentences to set Emma's mind at rest. And, with the extinction of this chief motive for dislike, Emma's attitude to Jane Fairfax undergoes an immediate and lasting change. Early in the next chapter, she is shown to be "more conscience-stricken about Jane Fairfax than she had often been"

(291). She reflects, "'I ought to have been more her friend.—She will never like me now. I have neglected her too long. But I will shew her greater attention than I have done'" (291).

Her first gesture—a source of relief at being spared an embarrassed Harriet as well as pleasure in Harriet's substitute—is to have Jane Fairfax as the eighth at her dinner-party for the Eltons. On this occasion she is as attentive to Jane Fairfax as Mrs Elton will allow and even lets pass the chance for a question about "the expedition and the expense of the Irish mails" (298). In the next few weeks, Emma has little opportunity for friendly gestures: Mrs Elton stands implacably between her and Jane Fairfax until such time as Jane Fairfax, whose turn it is to become jealous, begins to resist her overtures. Yet Emma does what she can. She tries to stop Frank Churchill passing the word 'Dixon' to Jane Fairfax. At Donwell Abbey, when Jane Fairfax can control her feelings no longer, Emma makes herself serviceable and then, "with the zeal of a friend" (363), meets her chief need by leaving her alone. On the next morning, at Box Hill, Jane Fairfax's jealousy of Emma becomes a serious force: but, throughout the illness that follows, Emma's kindly gestures are sustained in the face of bewildering affronts. When she finally hears how Jane Fairfax had been induced to enter into a secret engagement, in defiance of the standards of the day, Emma is full of pity for one so torn by love and also of regret for having "'often . . . contributed to make her unhappy'" (419). At their next meeting, Emma, though kept from speech by the presence of Mrs Elton, tries "to compress all her friendly and all her congratulatory sensations into a very, very earnest shake of the hand" (453).

If Jane Fairfax herself has so little influence on Emma's earlier picture of her, if the 'Jane Fairfax' of Emma's conscious mind is predominantly the thrall of Dixon and a threat to little Henry, we need to consider whether—in a novel where so much is seen through Emma's eyes—the *actual* Jane Fairfax is adequately portrayed. Her portrayal is certainly not adequate to the demands of those critics who would have all their characters fully 'realized' or of those who regard her as being set opposite to Emma in a leading, structural antithesis. The doctrine of 'realization' and the belief that Jane Austen intended such an antithesis meet in Dr Bradbrook who suggests, in the first place, that: 'The contrast between Jane Fairfax and Emma derives partly from the Richardsonian tradition in the novel which Jane Austen had outgrown. One of the conventions of this type of novel was that there should be a lively and [a?] quiet girl.' After instancing several such novels and arguing, rather tenuously, for a connection between liveliness and immorality, Dr Bradbrook claims that, upon the entrance of Jane Fairfax, the basic antithesis of the 'outgrown' Richardsonian convention begins to affect *Emma*:

> The introduction of the Richardsonian pattern a third of the way through the novel disturbs the delicate balance of comparisons and contrasts that has been established, and results in a character who never comes to life being inserted into the story.

This conclusion is re-asserted in a series of dismissive phrases: Mr Knightley's praise of Jane Fairfax is merely 'registered as information giving her a theoretical superiority'; 'she never establishes [a] vital, dramatic relationship with the heroine'; 'she only succeeds in making virtue, itself, appear unconvincing and unreal'.[4]

To the extent that this argument is governed by the notion that Jane Austen intended a major antithesis between Emma and Jane Fairfax, it has no solid basis. *Emma* is in no way bound by the suggestion—itself not indisputable—that Richardson, Fanny Burney, and the young Jane Austen relied on antithetical relationships between 'lively' girls and 'quiet' ones. And the ensuing value-judgements are quite as amenable to the construction that no such antithesis was intended as to the assumption that Jane Austen tried and failed. To the extent that such jargon as 'theoretical', 'vital', 'unconvincing', and 'unreal' implies a dependence upon a silent premise of 'realization', the ground at first appears more solid. For, in so far as that vague criterion requires that literary works each shed a radiant and individual light upon some aspect of our species and the world about us, there can be few who would cavil at it. Yet every great work establishes its unique necessities: and the role that *Emma* requires of Jane Fairfax inevitably precludes the kind of 'realization' apparent in those characters, like Mr Knightley and Frank Churchill, whom we frequently hear with our own ears even though we are usually obliged to look at them through the eyes of Emma Woodhouse.

Jane Austen's portrayal of Jane Fairfax is governed by opposed necessities. On the one hand, the reader must obviously be denied access to Jane Fairfax's true motives and can seldom, therefore, be allowed to hear her opinions, much less look through her eyes. As we have seen, there are occasions, especially in the chapter where her past history is recounted, when a statement of her former intentions can conceal her present hopes: "she had long resolved" (165) to turn governess at the age of twenty-one. Again, there are occasions when a seemingly indifferent subject permits Jane Fairfax to speak freely; but few subjects are really indifferent, as the narrow

4. Frank W. Bradbrook, *Jane Austen: 'Emma'*: all quotations from pp. 33-4.

74

escapes of her long conversation with John Knightley (293-7) make very plain. And, finally, there are occasions when the existence of an innocuous motive for speaking in a particular way conceals her true motive for doing so: she can speak freely of her pleasure in the proposed ball without drawing the least attention to her special cause for pleasure. It might be argued that, by granting him a flair for conscious ambiguity, Jane Austen can allow Frank Churchill to say a great deal without often endangering his secret. But this is not possible with a young woman who regards their secrecy as an unhappy necessity and cannot understand how he finds deviousness a pleasure in itself.

And yet, on the other hand, we must see enough of Jane Fairfax to understand that, here as elsewhere, Emma is misguided at first and very slow to change. Jane Fairfax is commended to us, in the first place, by the approval of others. Since no ground of prejudice is discernible, Mr Knightley's good opinion of her is a favourable sign. Again, as Dr Craik points out, the function of the amiable Campbells is very largely to 'make Jane seem more attractive than her role at Highbury gives her the chance to be'.[5] To this indirect evidence, which some would dismiss as 'theoretical', there must be added the testimony of those many occasions when Jane Fairfax's own actions and opinions are quoted by the invaluable Miss Bates. Through her we learn of little touches of thoughtfulness, of one who remains true to her first friends despite her new and glittering hopes.

But, just as Miss Bates' ignorance of those new hopes prevents her from appreciating the full extent of her niece's loyalty, so Jane Fairfax is always a stronger figure than her fellows are aware. There are always glimpses behind the smooth mask of her assumed reserve, as in that "deep blush of consciousness" and that "smile of secret delight" (243) which revive Emma's suspicions. But the second volume is far advanced before we properly understand how much it costs her to wear that mask so long. To so safe a listener as John Knightley, she can confess her loneliness and her fear of a narrowing future; and, in answer to his attempted reassurances, "a blush, a quivering lip, a tear in the eye, shewed that it was felt beyond a laugh" (294). At Donwell Abbey, Emma sees that her parting words, "'Oh! Miss Woodhouse, the comfort of being sometimes alone!'—seemed to burst from an overcharged heart, and to describe somewhat of the continual endurance to be practised by her, even towards some of those who loved her best" (363). And, finally, in her outburst against Frank Churchill at Box Hill, her withdrawing as soon as Emma arrives at Bates' the next morning,

5. W. A. Craik, *Jane Austen: The Six Novels*, p. 134.

and her distraught behaviour in the days that follow, that "over-charged heart" bursts the barriers of self-interest, courtesy, and even health itself.

From the first, however, Jane Fairfax has been free to speak of her future as a governess (without ever really knowing whether Frank Churchill will save her). Her natural repugnance for the prospect has been too readily identified with Jane Austen's own opinions: 'too readily' because, as a result, the peculiar intensity of Jane Fairfax's language has led critics out of the novel and into matters biographical. Certainly Jane Austen felt for the down-trodden governesses of her day, as when she remarked of Miss Allen, the governess at Godmersham, "By this time I suppose she is hard at it, governing away—poor creature! I pity her, tho' they *are* my neices" (*Letters*, p. 278). But though Jane Austen and Jane Fairfax are broadly of one mind, the latter is made to speak with an almost hysterical extravagance. At a time when the kindly Campbells are lamenting having given their foster-daughter "a taste of such enjoyments of ease and leisure as must now be relinquished" while yet remaining "glad to catch at any reasonable excuse for not hurrying on the wretched moment" (165), Jane Fairfax is already overwrought:

With the fortitude of a devoted noviciate, she had resolved at one-and-twenty to complete the sacrifice, and retire from all the pleasures of life, of rational intercourse, equal society, peace and hope, to penance and mortification for ever. (165)

This sentence, where the narrator speaks for Jane Fairfax in a manner which even Charlotte Brontë might have admired, is matched, much later, by the girl's own outcries about "'Offices for the sale—not quite of human flesh—but of human intellect'", about a "'governess-trade'" which, compared to the slave-trade, is "'widely different certainly as to the guilt of those who carry it on; but as to the greater misery of the victims, I do not know where it lies'" (300-1).

It must be a rare and misguided novice who—except in the worlds of Mrs Radcliffe and 'Monk' Lewis!—enters upon her vocation in the mood described. It must have been a rare governess whose miseries might properly be compared with the afflictions of a transported slave. These extravagant similitudes, moreover, cannot be matched in all the rest of *Emma*. Were they the comments of Jane Austen, *in propria persona*, one would expect rather more of her habitual concern for accuracy and restraint. But, if they are accepted as Jane Fairfax's one safe means of relieving her feelings, almost any hyperbole can be excused. Strong as it is, her repugnance

76

for becoming a governess is exacerbated by uncertainty about Frank Churchill, by dread of Mrs Churchill, and (in the second passage) by a growing intimacy, enforced by Mrs Elton, with the sombre future she can possibly expect.

In these passages one is reminded of Marianne Dashwood: but this memory is less serviceable for grounding an analogy than for stressing a difference. The author of *Emma* seldom relies on hyperbole even for registering mental torment. And, on a larger scale, the mature Jane Austen is too attentive to the endless variety of mankind to tolerate anything so factitious as the stiff antithesis between Marianne and Elinor upon which *Sense and Sensibility* is based. Emma's own foolish contrast between Harriet and Jane Fairfax (219) reminds us that the latter is only one of several characters who differ as significantly from each other as from the heroine. Through the ever-lessening distance between their actual selves and their roles in Emma's theatre of the mind, these subordinate characters provide our chief means of assessing Emma's many-sided emotional growth. Among these Harriets and Eltons, Jane Fairfax is only set apart by the force of her emotions and by the fact that one plain speech from her, one clear sight into her mind, would bring Emma's theatre in ruins about Jane Austen's ears. In winning our compassion for Jane Fairfax without ever succumbing to this constant danger, Jane Austen achieves an astonishing triumph of 'suggestive reticence'.[6]

III

On learning that Mr Elton is going to be married, Emma is faced at once with Mr Knightley's knowing comments and with a sublime instance of Miss Bates' promiscuous goodwill: " 'It is such a happiness when good people get together—and they always do' " (175). But these trifles are supplanted by graver irritations. Emma's amused satisfaction in the discovery that "Mr. Elton could not have suffered long" (177) does not survive her encounters with that gentleman who, "caring nothing for Miss Woodhouse, and defying Miss Smith" (181), lays himself open to a just charge of "pique and pretension" (182). There is a corresponding change in Emma's attitude to the unknown Miss Hawkins. At first she is seen as a blessing, a means of ensuring that "former intimacy might sink without remark" (183). Gradually, however, Elton's "vaunted claims and disdain of Harriet" (183) induce a harsher mood, and

6. 'There are . . . few finer examples in fiction of suggestive reticence than Jane Austen's treatment of Jane Fairfax': Harold Child, 'Jane Austen', *Cambridge History of English Literature*, Vol. xii (1915), p. 240.

Emma enters upon a series of bitter comparisons between Miss Hawkins and Miss Smith. There is, of course, a small matter of ten thousand pounds. But once that is set aside, in a single cavalier phrase, Miss Hawkins' other advantages are easily turned against her. Given that Emma is interpreting the "vaunted claims" of a Philip Elton, she may well suspect such euphemisms as "in the law line" (183), so constant an emphasis on the two carriages. One might wish, even so, that Emma had reserved judgement until Augusta herself appeared (and, as it happens, surpassed her most savage hopes). But Jane Austen knows her heroine too well for that: "Of the lady, individually, Emma thought very little" (183).

Emma is keenly aware that Harriet will be distressed by the news of the marriage and she wishes, if possible, to soften the blow. But, remembering the winged pattens of Miss Bates, the village Mercury, she is not much surprised when Harriet arrives "with just the heated, agitated look which hurrying thither with a full heart was likely to give" (177). As it transpires, Harriet has quite another tale to tell.

In this, the longest speech she allows her, Jane Austen captures the quintessence of Harriet. Of her general incoherence and particular illiteracies, it is enough to say, with Dr Chapman, that 'Mrs. Goddard no doubt had done her best' (178, editor's note). But her obsequiousness towards Miss Woodhouse goes so deep as to cast doubts on her sincerity: could even a Harriet, from sweet stupidity alone, feel the need to apologize so profusely for encountering the Martins in a shop? A single item of firm evidence might be decisive: but one is left with a handful of ambiguous phrases, a lingering suspicion, and some uneasy doubts about one's own suspicious mind. One can be certain, however, that Harriet's interest in Robert Martin has never lapsed entirely: "'Oh! Miss Woodhouse, I would rather done any thing than have had it happen: and yet, you know, there was a sort of satisfaction in seeing him behave so pleasantly and so kindly'" (179). (Through his being kept in Harriet's mind, moreover, he is being kept in ours: the seemingly casual report [232-3] of his having dined with the Coxes is another case in point.) Martin, of course, is not Harriet's only lost hero. As she wavers between him and the gallant Elton, much as she will waver over the destination of a parcel, she positively invites Emma's reflection that love alone can "occupy the many vacancies of Harriet's mind" (183).

When Harriet's tale of her encounter with the Martins goes on and on, Emma, fearing a serious revival of interest, uses Elton as a corrective by "hurry[ing] on the news, which she had meant to give with so much tender caution" (180). But, when Elton's importance with Harriet revives, Emma dares not use Robert Martin for a like purpose. By now, indeed, he arouses real doubts and hesitations:

The young man's conduct, and his sister's, seemed the result of real feeling, and she could not but pity them. As Harriet described it, there had been an interesting mixture of wounded affection and genuine delicacy in their behaviour. But she had believed them to be well meaning, worthy people before; and what difference did this make in the evils of the connection? It was folly to be disturbed by it. Of course, he must be sorry to lose her— they must be all sorry. Ambition, as well as love, had probably been mortified. They might all have hoped to rise by Harriet's acquaintance: and besides, what was the value of Harriet's description?—so easily pleased— so little discerning;—what signified her praise? (179-80)

There is nothing novel in Emma's verdict, in the obstinacy with which she clings to it, or in her willingness to mix fanciful slurs with misguided principles. Her new hesitancy is felt rather in the potent concessions that "could not but" escape her: in her references to "real feeling", "wounded affection and genuine delicacy"; in the astonishing admission of "as well as love"; and, perhaps strongest of all, in the word "interesting" which, at that time, usually reflected a more serious concern than it does today.[7] The upshot is that, while Emma can tell herself that "it was folly to be disturbed by it", she is not the less disturbed.

Emma eventually comforts herself in the belief that "a twelvemonth might pass without their being thrown together again" (180). But only a few days later, Elizabeth Martin writes Harriet a note "in the very style to touch; a small mixture of reproach, with a great deal of kindness" (184). Harriet cannot decide how to answer it and—in a most revealing phrase—wishes "to do more than she dared to confess" (185). Emma also weighs it long and doubtfully: "Absolute neglect of the mother and sisters, when invited to come,

7. Johnson's definitions unequivocally favour the older, stronger force of the word [*Dictionary* (*see* 'interest')] as do most of the many instances in *Emma* (e.g. 40, 163, 189, 261, 358, 417). There is a striking instance in 'Lady Susan', where Sir Reginald writes in perturbation to his son: "You must be sensible that as an only son & the representative of an ancient Family, your conduct in Life is most interesting to your connections. In the very important concern of Marriage especially, there is everything at stake" (*Minor Works*, p. 260). And, just after the death of her brother Edward's wife, Jane Austen writes to Cassandra at Godmersham: "Your account of Lizzy is very interesting. Poor child! One must hope the impression *will* be strong, and yet one's heart aches for a dejected mind of eight years old" (*Letters*, p. 221).

Yet there are occasions in *Emma* (e.g. 181) when "interesting" is used with those coy overtones which—originating perhaps in Restoration plays— led eventually to the well-known Victorian euphemism for pregnancy, 'an interesting condition'.

would be ingratitude. It must not be: and yet the danger of a renewal of the acquaintance!" (185). After resolving to have Harriet pay a purely formal visit to the Martins, Emma acknowledges to herself that "there was something in it which her own heart could not approve—something of ingratitude, merely glossed over" (185). On the day itself, Emma is further troubled by what she sees of the Abbey Mill Farm, with its air of unpretentious prosperity, and by Harriet's account of her reception there. She decides, accordingly, to go home by way of Randalls for "a little consolation" (187). When they arrive there, only to find that the Westons are at Hartfield, Emma's unusual fit of ill-temper reflects the increasing strain of defending an untenable position against an uneasy conscience. It is not the first time that Emma's heart has given better counsel than her avowed principles: but it is almost the last time she will allow those principles to prevail.

Even as Emma leans back "to indulge her murmurs, or to reason them away; probably a little of both—such being the commonest process of a not ill-disposed mind" (187-8), the carriage is stopped by the Westons. Frank Churchill, they announce, is to arrive next day. Emma cannot resist such news, and shares their joy. And she is quick to hear a veiled suggestion that she figures prominently in Weston's plans for his son. The brilliant ironies foreshadowed in these empty hopes are matched, in the same moment, by the immediate ironies of a conclusion in which nothing is concluded. As Emma's recent problems vanish from her mind, the very countryside reflects her altered mood:

. . . James and his horses seemed not half so sluggish as before. When she looked at the hedges, she thought the elder at least must soon be coming out; and when she turned round to Harriet, she saw something like a look of spring, a tender smile even there. (189)

Unfortunately for Emma, this miraculous flush of spring has escaped Harriet's attention: "'Will Mr. Frank Churchill pass through Bath as well as Oxford?'—was a question, however, which did not augur much" (189).

IV

At Hartfield next morning, a pattern for the future is unobtrusively laid down. Having no reason to suspect ulterior motives, Weston interprets his son's unexpectedly early arrival in Highbury as evidence of an attitude to life as insouciant as his own. The son not only avails himself of the excuse but actually strikes a profit on the whole exchange:

"I told you all that he would be here before the time named. I remembered what I used to do myself. One cannot creep upon a journey; one cannot help getting on faster than one has planned; and the pleasure of coming in upon one's friends before the look-out begins, is worth a great deal more than any little exertion it needs."

"It is a great pleasure where one can indulge in it," said the young man, "though there are not many houses that I should presume on so far; but in coming *home* I felt I might do any thing."

The word *home* made his father look on him with fresh complacency. (190-1)

When Mrs Weston, in her turn, misjudges her step-son's intention by imposing on him an attitude of her own, the point is stated almost explicitly. She asks him to decide where they should walk—and he naturally fixes on Highbury. Now "Highbury, with Mrs. Weston, stood for Hartfield; and she trusted to its bearing the same construction with him. They walked thither directly" (196). On this occasion, Frank Churchill finds no way of regaining his real end, and Emma is flattered to find him paying her so prompt a second visit.

Through the cumulative effect of such little misconstructions, each of the novel's leading figures builds up his own 'Frank Churchill'. And, because the young man pays close heed to their notions of him, he is able to get a good deal of his own way without being seen to do so. (Mr Knightley, of course, is implacably hostile: but he still misreads the evidence.) All this is not to suggest that Frank Churchill is infallible. He blunders at times, most notably in the matter of Perry's carriage. He lays himself open to censure, most notably by providing so flimsy an excuse for going suddenly to London. He fails dismally in his attempts to manage Mr Woodhouse. And, most important of all, he participates in the local habit of misconstruction by supposing that Emma guesses his real object.

This web of misconstruction gives the critic a delicate task. One may easily stand so close as to lose the advantages of perspective. Professor Wright, for example, is prepared—though surely only in a moment of forgetfulness—to take his stance beside the characters themselves. Frank Churchill, he says, 'goes to London for the sole purpose of getting his hair cut. This is a piece of frivolity, of wanton lightness, which even Emma can recognize.'[8] Yet, when the critic stands off at a distance, he may easily lose the precise 'note' of the novel, the particular ambience that marks *Emma* as unique. Only so, one would imagine, could Frank Churchill be condemned in terms more apt for Richardson's Lovelace or for the supposedly 'gay' Lothario of Rowe's *Fair Penitent*: condemned as a creature of 'treacherous egotism'; as worthy peer to an Emma who can be 'coldly cruel,

8. Andrew H. Wright, *Jane Austen's Novels: A Study in Structure*, p. 161.

which even Mrs. Elton never is'; as a character essential to a novel in which 'the problem is nothing less than original sin—the dry destructiveness of egotism'.[9]

If one is to judge properly of the relationships that evolve between Frank Churchill and his fellows, one must accept the advantages of after-knowledge. But, even while knowing more than any of the characters, one must make allowance for their knowing less. And, again, the nuances of Jane Austen's artistry are most fully discernible if one can allow the novel to unfold *as if* for the first time. No single 'ideal' standpoint can serve such disparate ends: one must shift ground as occasion requires without forgetting that one is shifting ground. Like most critical precepts, this is easier to expound than to enact; like them, again, it assumes its full meaning only when it is enacted.

In the pages given over to Emma's first conversation with Frank Churchill, there are moments when Jane Austen's narrative method is stretched to its limit. In much of what passes between them, it is true, no special difficulties arise. When Frank Churchill is showering fulsome compliments on all about him, there are frequent reminders that the third-person commentary lays no claim to omniscience but only represents what Emma is thinking the while. Thus her first suspicions and her increasing gratification are shown clearly to be hers: "Emma was directly sure that he knew how to make himself agreeable" (191); "if it were a falsehood, it was a pleasant one, and pleasantly handled" (191); "she must see more of him to understand his ways; at present she only felt they were agreeable" (192); "Emma remained very well pleased with this beginning of the acquaintance" (195). The narrator speaks for Emma once again when, just after she has praised Jane Fairfax as "'a very elegant young woman'", we are told:

> He agreed to it, but with so quiet a "Yes," as inclined her almost to doubt his real concurrence; and yet there must be a very distinct sort of elegance for the fashionable world, if Jane Fairfax could be thought only ordinarily gifted with it. (194)

The Emma who had been half-impressed by Elton's florid compliments is unmoved by this cautious (but sincere) "Yes"; the Emma who has grown up in Highbury marvels a little at the fashionable world; and the cue-phrase, "inclined her almost to doubt", leaves us in no doubt that the response is hers indeed.

But, whenever Frank Churchill is considering how he can gain

9. Mark Schorer, 'The Humiliation of Emma Woodhouse' in Ian Watt (ed.), *Jane Austen*, pp. 107, 111.

access to Jane Fairfax, there are none of these unequivocal cue-phrases. Thus, when Mr Weston announces that he must get about his business but that "'he need not hurry any body else'", the narrator suavely comments that "his son, too well bred to hear the hint, rose immediately also"; and the son then announces his obligation of calling on "'a family of the name of Fairfax . . . though Fairfax, I believe, is not the proper name'" (193). A second and subtler example occurs a little earlier:

> Their subjects in general were such as belong to an opening acquaintance. On his side were the inquiries,—"Was she a horse-woman?—Pleasant rides?—Pleasant walks?—Had they a large neighbourhood?—Highbury, perhaps, afforded society enough?—There were several very pretty houses in and about it.—Balls—had they balls?—Was it a musical society?" (191)

In both cases, to begin with, the narrator's comments fall short of the whole truth. Frank Churchill ignores his father's deliberate hint that he should stay at Hartfield not because he is "too well bred to hear" it but because he sees a chance of calling on Jane Fairfax. And, though the other conversation deals in such subjects "as belong to an opening acquaintance", Frank Churchill is not just exchanging pleasantries. With his last two questions, especially, there can be little doubt that Jane Fairfax is in his mind. On his second morning in Highbury, he initiates the idea of a ball at the Crown, arguing "like a young man very much bent on dancing" and, ironically, exposing himself to Emma's inferences about "his indifference to a confusion of rank" (198). And surely it is he who sets the Coles' guests a-dancing. At the time we are told only that "the proposal of dancing—originating nobody exactly knew where—was . . . effectually promoted" (229). But Frank Churchill had previously broached the possibility of dancing that evening (208); and, on the following morning, he as much as tells Jane Fairfax that the dancing had stopped too soon to meet his purpose (242).

The inadequacy of the narrator's comments would be of no special importance if, as so often, they merely represented Emma's thoughts. But there is no real warrant for interpreting them in this way. In the first example, admittedly, the phrase "too well bred to hear the hint" is immediately preceded by remarks which are detached from their speaker, Mr Weston, by what might be called a third-person rendering of direct speech: "'He must be going. He had business at the Crown about his hay . . . but he need not hurry any body else.'" But, while this form of expression gently stresses the hearers rather than the speaker, it does not single out Emma from among the other hearers or suggest that she is putting any special interpretation upon what is said. The most striking feature of the second example is the omission of Emma's side of the conversation. The only definite sign that she, personally, is engaged lies in the transition from "'Had they a large neighbourhood?'" to "'Highbury, perhaps, afforded society enough?'" The latter question follows from Emma's being obliged (as we know she would be) to answer the former in the negative. (The transition from questions about riding to one about walking is similar in kind but less definite in its effect.) Here, too, there is no clear sign that the comment on "their subjects in general" is Emma's own.

When Dr Chapman discusses the phrase, "too well bred to hear the hint", he concludes that we *should* regard the narrator as speaking for Emma. Disturbed, nevertheless, by the lack of an unequivocal warrant for this interpretation, he wonders whether Jane Austen is 'deliberately throwing dust in our eyes' but then decides otherwise: 'I think the slip inadvertent'.[10] Presumably all novels contain inadvertent slips; and *Emma* is not flawless. Jane Austen's family were quick to notice that the orchard at the Abbey Mill Farm blossoms at midsummer (360: cf. *Life*, p. 307). And, as Dr Chapman shows, Jane Austen rather than Mrs Elton is guilty of misquoting Gray: for Mrs Elton, alas, is a trifle more accurate than Catherine Morland (*Emma*, 282 and note; cf. *Northanger Abbey*, p. 15 and note). Yet, as Dr Chapman himself remarks, *Emma* is uncommonly free of inadvertencies; and arguments from inadvertency ought surely to be regarded as our last resort.

Another interpretation emerges if one tries to imagine how *else* Jane Austen might have met her difficulties. If either comment had unmistakably been given the full weight of the narrator's authority, Jane Austen would have defeated her own purposes: it would have been idle to put significant little questions into Frank Churchill's mouth during a conversation which the reader had virtually been instructed to ignore; and it would have been entirely misleading to instruct us that Frank Churchill's behaviour is governed, at this point, merely by good breeding. But suppose, conversely, that the comments had unmistakably been shown as Emma's. 'It seemed to Emma [the text might run] that their subjects in general were such as belong to an opening acquaintance'; or, again, 'The son, she supposed, was too well bred to hear the hint.' As we have seen, simple cue-phrases like these can serve, even in this intricate chapter, when Frank Churchill is talking more at large. But when his subject is dangerously near home, Jane Austen cannot afford to be so definite: if we were encouraged to begin inquiring into Emma's exact meaning, we might end by seriously questioning Frank

10. R. W. Chapman, *Jane Austen: Facts and Problems*, p. 206.

Churchill's motives; and it is too soon for that. In circumstances as demanding as any she has to face, Jane Austen keeps her reader exactly where she wants him. She does so, moreover, without exceeding a novelist's just prerogative: for—as the example of Conrad reminds us—a novelist is entitled to tell his reader as much as he chooses when he chooses provided he does not involve himself in contradictions or in pointless complications.

Jane Austen's task grows more straightforward soon after this first meeting between Emma and Frank Churchill is brought safely to an end. Accompanied by Mrs Weston, they spend the next morning strolling about Highbury. As soon as the question can seem natural, Jane Austen has Emma rather idly ask him about his earlier acquaintance with Jane Fairfax. At first he avoids the question by turning into Ford's. After a little thought, however, he returns to the point and, having dexterously established that Jane Fairfax has said nothing untoward, makes a suitably guarded reply:

"Then I will speak the truth, and nothing suits me so well. I met her frequently at Weymouth. I had known the Campbells a little in town; and at Weymouth we were very much in the same set. Col. Campbell is a very agreeable man, and Mrs. Campbell a friendly, warm-hearted woman. I like them all." (200-1)

With this crucial question asked and—to all appearances— answered, the narrative can flow more freely; and the further it flows, the easier its course becomes.

By the end of the morning, they have seen most of the village, including the Crown, where Frank Churchill speaks enthusiastically of dancing, and the vicarage, where he speaks (sentimentally enough but more sincerely than they know) of love in a cottage. They have appraised Miss Fairfax's complexion, her reserve, and her musician-ship. And, after an almost accidental beginning, Frank Churchill has re-awakened Emma's fancy by telling her how curiously Mr Dixon's love of music had taken precedence over his affection for Miss Campbell. In all this time, Frank Churchill says nothing that is not closely related to his dominant purpose. Yet Emma is utterly deceived: "after walking together so long, and thinking so much alike, Emma felt herself so well acquainted with him, that she could hardly believe it to be only their second meeting" (203). The implica-tions of a relationship established on such uneasy foundations will occupy us shortly. But my immediate point is still one of narrative method. In the phrase, "thinking so much alike", the narrator must obviously be speaking for Emma: and the sequel, "Emma felt . . .", confirms that it is so. Accordingly, when the next chapter opens upon ironies guarded by the familiar "seemed" and "appeared"

(205), Jane Austen can be said, if only by her standards, to have relaxed.

V

Throughout his first visit to Highbury, Frank Churchill himself remains firm of purpose and swift of resource; and the more serious possibilities latent in his intrigue are not yet allowed intrude. This being so, the business of distinguishing, moment by moment, what he is about (which makes part of one's pleasure as a reader—or, presumably, a re-reader) need not occupy us here. Let us confine ourselves to two more episodes, instances not only of his skill itself but also of the amusement he finds in exercising it.

These qualities are nowhere more evident than when he is transforming a near-blunder into a tactical advantage. At one point during the Coles' dinner-party, Emma's attention is engaged by her host. When she turns back to Frank Churchill, she finds him "looking intently across the room at Miss Fairfax" (222). Upon her interrupting him, he starts a little and then thanks her: he had, he says, been staring rudely at Miss Fairfax's extraordinary hairstyle. He must ask her "'whether it is an Irish fashion'", and Emma shall see whether she colours at the suggestion. Unfortunately for Emma, he is so "improvident" as to stand "exactly in front of Miss Fairfax, [and] she could absolutely distinguish nothing" (222). In other circumstances, even Emma might have been surprised by his finding a seat beside Miss Fairfax and remaining with her until the evening's music supervenes. But Emma's attention is distracted. Full of pride in her acuteness and satisfaction in her discovery, Mrs Weston seizes this moment to tell Emma that Mr Knightley may intend to marry Jane Fairfax. Although we have seen how Emma responds to *this* suggestion, it is worth noticing how prettily the two incidents are juxtaposed. Even as they argue about Jane Fairfax's possible future, her real future is being shaped before their unseeing eyes.

The next morning brings Frank Churchill's most brilliant hour. While Emma is waiting outside Ford's for Harriet, who is "hanging over muslins and changing her mind" (233), she sees Mrs Weston and Frank Churchill in the distance. She promptly repeats Mrs Weston's earlier mistake ("they were walking into Highbury;—to Hartfield of course": 233), but is soon informed that they are actually going to Bates' to hear the new instrument. Frank Churchill, it emerges, has 'reminded' Mrs Weston that she had promised to do so. He now urges Mrs Weston to go on alone, saying that he would prefer to remain with Miss Woodhouse. Always the gentleman, however, he yields politely to their polite resistance and, "with the hope of Hartfield to reward him" (235), goes with Mrs Weston.

86

Success soon breeds success. When the others decide that Miss Woodhouse (and, of course, Miss Smith) must be asked to join the party, he lets Miss Bates and Mrs Weston convey the invitation: he would naturally be glad to go; but Mrs Bates' spectacles must first be mended. With old Mrs Bates dozing beside the fire and with the assurance that Miss Bates' garrulousness will not only delay the others but also serve warning of their return, he and Jane Fairfax are allowed a "stolen Interveiw".[11]

"The appearance of the little sitting-room as they entered, was tranquillity itself" (240). If his repairs to the spectacles are still unfinished, he is ready with an excuse. If his comment that they have returned "'at least ten minutes earlier than I had calculated'" expresses less pleasure than his manner suggests, there is no one to suppose so. And if Miss Fairfax, who is "intent on her pianoforté", seems ill at ease, Emma assumes that "she had not yet possessed the instrument long enough to touch it without emotion" (240). Frank Churchill's veiled annoyance soon gives way to a mood of exhilaration. In speech after speech, he leads the party at large to suppose that he is politely admiring Colonel Campbell's gift; has Emma convinced that he is talking about Dixon; and, all the while, is addressing Jane Fairfax on his own behalf:

"I heard a good deal of Col. Campbell's taste at Weymouth; and the softness of the upper notes I am sure is exactly what he and *all that party* would particularly prize. I dare say, Miss Fairfax, that he either gave his friend very minute directions, or wrote to Broadwood himself. Do not you think so?" (241)

"What felicity it is to hear a tune again which *has* made one happy!— If I mistake not that was danced at Weymouth." (242)

"He knew Miss Fairfax could have no music here. I honour that part of the attention particularly; it shews it to have been so thoroughly from the heart. Nothing hastily done; nothing incomplete. True affection only could have prompted it." (242)

When Emma whispers that Miss Fairfax will understand him, he replies, as well he may, "'I hope she does. . . . I am not in the least ashamed of my meaning'" (243).

Secure all this while in one's after-knowledge, one might allow a legitimate amusement at seeing Emma so thoroughly deceived to swell into condescension or even scorn. To allow this, however, is to over-simplify. A subtle but profound change in the attitude of so perceptive a critic as Professor Trilling testifies to Jane Austen's

11. In 'Sanditon', we are told that "Charlotte c^d not but think of the extreme difficulty which secret Lovers must have in finding a proper spot for their stolen Interveiws" (*Minor Works*, p. 427).

ability to defend her heroine against our possible excesses. In his best-known essay on Jane Austen, he declares, in passing, that Emma is 'made to stand at bay to our adverse judgement through virtually the whole novel' but that 'we are never permitted to close in for the kill—some unnamed quality in the girl, some trait of vivacity or will, erects itself into a moral principle, or at least a vital principle, and frustrates our moral blood-lust'.[12] In his essay on *Emma* itself, first published three years later, he takes up a remark from one of Newman's letters and maintains that 'the real question about Emma [is] whether or not we will find it in our hearts to be kind to her'.[13] And he goes on to argue that, for all her faults, we cannot really do otherwise. Now, in some abstract sense, these two comments make the same point: that we may feel tempted to judge Emma more severely than we are actually permitted to do. But consider how radically the notion of feeling 'kind' to Emma qualifies the harsher language of the earlier comment, with its metaphor from bear-baiting and its talk of 'moral blood-lust'. When he is more intimately in touch with *Emma*, it seems, Professor Trilling responds more fully to those subtle processes in the novel which work against much of the more obvious evidence and leave us well disposed towards its heroine.

Take the important and extremely complex case of Emma's suspicions about Jane Fairfax and Mr Dixon. As we have seen, these suspicions, in themselves, are not entirely without warrant. But further, more serious questions arise when Emma passes them on to Frank Churchill. So far from attempting to excuse her on the ground that she soon repents this action, Jane Austen shows most clearly that it is a long time before Emma's repentance amounts to anything more than an erratic impulse of regret. At her first opportunity for reflection, her pangs of conscience are easily assuaged by rationalizations and self-flattery:

She doubted whether she had not transgressed the duty of woman by woman, in betraying her suspicions of Jane Fairfax's feelings to Frank Churchill. It was hardly right; but it had been so strong an idea, that it would escape her, and his submission to all that she told, was a compliment to her penetration which made it difficult for her to be quite certain that she ought to have held her tongue. (231)

Emma's regrets are naturally stronger when she actually sees Jane Fairfax standing at her piano and supposes (more truly than she

---

12. Lionel Trilling, 'Jane Austen and *Mansfield Park*', *Partisan Review*, Vol. xxi (1954), p. 493.
13. Lionel Trilling, '*Emma* and the Legend of Jane Austen' in *Beyond Culture: Essays on Literature and Learning*, p. 37; first published as an Introduction to *Emma*, Riverside edn, Boston 1957.

knows) that she is thinking of the donor: "Emma could not but pity such feelings, whatever their origin, and could not but resolve never to expose them to her neighbour again" (240-1). Although her good resolution comes too late, her pity seems genuine enough, especially when it issues in an attempt to stop Frank Churchill from dropping any more of his sly hints: "'It is not fair,' said Emma in a whisper, 'mine was a random guess. Do not distress her'" (241). When Frank Churchill goes on to remark that "'true affection only could have prompted [the gift]'", Emma is ashamed of being amused. But, when she notices Jane Fairfax's "smile of secret delight", she gives fresh credence to her suspicions and, in the name of the proprieties, feels only "'half ashamed'" (243).

By the time of the word-game at Hartfield, a hundred pages later, Emma is "really ashamed of having ever imparted" (350) her suspicions, though still not of having harboured them. And, by the time of that "very long, and melancholy" (421) July evening which marks the most sombre point in the whole novel, Emma at last appreciates how badly she has behaved. Her misery increased because she can make no adequate redress, she acknowledges that, by knowing Jane Fairfax:

... as she ought, and as she might, she must have been preserved from the abominable suspicions of an improper attachment to Mr. Dixon, which she had not only so foolishly fashioned and harboured herself, but had so unpardonably imparted; an idea which she greatly feared had been made a subject of material distress to the delicacy of Jane's feelings, by the levity or carelessness of Frank Churchill's. Of all the sources of evil surrounding the former, since her coming to Highbury, she was persuaded that she must herself have been the worst. She must have been a perpetual enemy. (421)

But these developments must await their time. Having seen the affair in its worst light and having seen how firmly Jane Austen rejects any easy extenuations, we must consider how, even from the first, she gives it all another aspect.

In this more genial aspect, Emma's imparting of her suspicions is shown to stem from her belief in a special relationship—so to call it for a moment—between Frank Churchill and herself. As we have seen, both Emma and the Westons have long regarded him as a possible suitor. And, during his visit, as he afterwards admits:

"My behaviour to Miss Woodhouse indicated, I believe, more than it ought.—In order to assist a concealment so essential to me, I was led on to make more than an allowable use of the sort of intimacy into which we were immediately thrown." (438)

Out of the motives she cannot but impute to such behaviour and out of her knowledge (such as it is) of her own feelings, Emma soon accepts that their relationship is indeed a special one. And, if *we* are shown a number of little danger signals, they are such as no one present could possibly decipher:

> They were soon joined by some of the gentlemen; and the very first of the early was Frank Churchill. In he walked, the first and the handsomest; and *after paying his compliments en passant to Miss Bates and her niece*, made his way directly to the opposite side of the circle, where sat Miss Woodhouse; and till he could find a seat by her, would not sit at all. (220; my italics)

My phrase, 'a special relationship', was not intended as a coy periphrasis but as a means of deferring the last of the many distinctions required by this complex set of issues. On its more obvious and less important level, the level on which Emma understands it, her relationship with Frank Churchill is one of love. From the time of their first long stroll together until shortly after he is recalled to Enscombe, Emma pauses regularly to excogitate his feelings and to celebrate her own. Simply because of his ulterior motives, his manner towards her conforms precisely to her notion that love consists in treating one's beloved as " 'always first and always right' " (84). He comes constantly to Hartfield, expresses a close interest in all her doings, defers to her most fanciful opinions, and even pauses to admire the genius of a perfectly commonplace phrase: " 'Miss Woodhouse, you have the art of giving pictures in a few words. Exquisite, quite exquisite!' " (249-50). Whenever he acts otherwise, as in going so unexpectedly to London or in valuing dancing at so extreme a rate—whenever indeed he acts in a way she cannot understand—Emma solemnly asks herself if he is worthy of her love. But, in general, he is a veritable Prince Charming.

Her estimate of her own feelings is even more absurd. After his departure, she "continued to entertain no doubt of her being in love" (264). And, weeks later, she is surprised to discover that passion has not left her inarticulate:

> "—Am I unequal to speaking his name at once before all these people? Is it necessary for me to use any roundabout phrase?—Your Yorkshire friend—your correspondent in Yorkshire;—that would be the way, I suppose, if I were very bad.—No, I can pronounce his name without the smallest distress. I certainly get better and better." (297)

Regarding love as she does, Emma cannot—and would not choose to—appreciate how little her feelings have to do with love as it is *commonly* understood. Her most constant concern is that others should be noticing his attentions to her. Her chief doubt is for "how soon it might be necessary for her to throw coldness into her air" (212). Her intention of never marrying is quite unshaken even when she thinks he is on the point of a declaration. Her decision to make him over to Harriet "'when we cease to care for each other as we do now'" (267) brings this splendid episode to an appropriate conclusion. And, as she contemplates her future, her tone is that of a child recovering from measles: "'I shall do very well again after a little while—and then, it will be a good thing over; for they say every body is in love once in their lives, and I shall have been let off easily'" (265).

Beneath the light-hearted raillery that is directed at Emma's version of their relationship, a deeper irony begins to stir. While her attention is given to their supposed attachment, she is becoming attached to him in quite another way:

"—She received my attentions with an easy, friendly, goodhumoured playfulness, which exactly suited me. We seemed to understand each other. From our relative situation, those attentions were her due, and were felt to be so." (438)

In trying to discredit this comment by impugning Frank Churchill's motives, Mr Knightley ignores the evidence of Emma's behaviour. For most of her life, she had found in Miss Taylor "one to whom she could speak every thought as it arose, and who had such an affection for her as could never find fault" (6). And yet, as the novel proceeds, it is remarkable how many of Emma's leading ideas, especially the indecorous ones, are never discussed with Mrs Weston. Her opposition to Robert Martin, her plans for Elton, her suspicions about Dixon, and—on another plane—her attachment to Frank Churchill are notable examples. Perhaps we are to accept Miss Taylor's removal from Hartfield as sufficient explanation. Perhaps Emma's original phrase, "speak *every* thought as it arose", is an exaggeration marking her keen sense of loss. Or perhaps Jane Austen could not afford to expose Emma's wilder fancies to Mrs Weston's gentle commonsense. At all events, Mrs Weston no longer fully satisfies one of Emma's most genuine needs; Harriet Smith has proved a lamentable substitute; and, without quite realizing what she is doing, Emma discovers in Frank Churchill an intimate friend and perfect confidant.[14]

This process begins at their first meeting. When Frank Churchill announces his obligation of calling on Miss Fairfax, his father responds, with his usual enthusiasm, "'I remember you knew her at Weymouth, and a fine girl she is'" and goes on to warn that "'any want of attention to her *here* should be carefully avoided'"

14. Mr Robert Liddell argues that Emma and Frank Churchill treat each other unceremoniously because they regard each other as brother and sister: *see The Novels of Jane Austen*, pp. 95-7.

because "'she is with a poor old grandmother, who has barely enough to live on'" (194). Though this hint, as he calls it, and his remark about "a fine girl" are thoroughly well meant, they show a degree of familiarity that even he would scarcely risk in other company. He obviously feels that he can speak quite openly at Hartfield and that his son is an addition to *both* families. Never loth to follow such an example, Emma speaks generously of Jane Fairfax's elegance and then offers a second useful hint: "'I am afraid you will not hear her at all, for she has an aunt who never holds her tongue'" (194). When Mr Woodhouse, who addresses Frank Churchill throughout as "'Sir'", speaks of the "'very agreeable young lady'" he is to visit and of the "'very worthy people'" (194) with whom she is staying, his more formal manner sets the familiarity of his neighbour and his daughter in a decorous perspective.

But Frank Churchill admits no such perspective. When he meets Emma next morning, he thanks her warmly for her hint: "'If the talking aunt had taken me quite by surprize, it must have been the death of me'" (198-9). He then speaks emphatically of Miss Fairfax's "'most deplorable want of complexion'" (199). Conscious only of his freedom of speech and guessing nothing of his motives, Emma encourages further confidences. His tale of the man who put Miss Fairfax's music before his duty to his fiancée evokes the comment that, "'We shall know more about them all, in half an hour, from you, than Miss Fairfax would have vouchsafed in half a year'" (202); and they continue with an increasingly plain-spoken discussion of that singular incident. At first Frank Churchill insists that Miss Campbell did not seem to mind. But then he sees how he can turn the conversation to his own advantage and disingenuously admits that he had no way of knowing what might have passed behind the scenes: "'I can only say that there was smoothness outwardly'" (202-3). Leaving Emma to make what she likes of this insinuation, he next seizes an opportunity to discover her real opinion of Jane Fairfax. Upon such encouragement, she confesses to a long-standing dislike. A wiser woman than Emma would be deceived by his carefully phrased reply and could be pardoned for supposing that "he perfectly agreed with her" (203).

When they meet at the Coles' dinner-party, the conversation around them is all of the new pianoforte. Like Mrs Weston, Emma is quick to suspect that Colonel Campbell cannot be the donor because he would have made no mystery of the gift. She sees Frank Churchill smiling and asks why he does so. Sensing that Emma may suspect the truth, he temporizes for a little and then boldly asks whom else she has in mind. After a tentative gesture towards Mrs Dixon, Emma meets his challenge and rehearses her real suspicions, chapter and verse, with no proviso except that the intentions of both parties might well have remained perfectly honourable throughout. Frank Churchill, admittedly, is in no position to object. But his previous willingness to exploit Emma's misapprehension ("'there was smoothness outwardly'") and his subsequent amusement ("'I, simple I, saw nothing but the fact'": 218) suggest that he is well content to have Dixon as his shield. And so he merely continues to praise Emma for her insight.

In the drawing-room afterwards, before he comes to join her, Emma reflects on what has passed. She tacitly re-affirms her point about honourable intentions by fancying how glad Jane Fairfax would be made "by the surrender of all the dangerous pleasure of knowing herself beloved by the husband of her friend" (219). She next decides that she must say nothing to Jane Fairfax about the pianoforte: "she felt too much in the secret herself, to think the appearance of curiosity or interest fair, and therefore purposely kept at a distance" (220). Set beside her earlier indiscretion, Emma's delicacy on this lesser point shows how thoroughly she trusts Frank Churchill: it is as if she had confided only in a second self. She learns otherwise next morning when, ignoring her pleas for silence, he lets fall a series of broad hints about Mr Dixon. Even though Jane Fairfax's "smile of secret delight" seems to confirm her worst suspicions, Emma is not appeased. Not knowing how thoroughly she is being deceived, she will still nourish the belief that he 'loves' her. But their short-lived intimacy is already at an end and she never confides in him again.

Emma's many-faceted relationship with Frank Churchill, the centre of attention in this second volume, can be epitomized at last in the rise and fall of her belief that he is "amiable". Etymology alone might suggest that this is an interesting word for her to use of him. According to *The Oxford English Dictionary*, its true progenitor was 'amicus' but its meaning, in both French and English, has always been influenced by a popular association with 'amare'. As a synonym for 'amicable', it was used as early as 1350 but had ceased to be used of persons by about 1500. (It survived as an epithet applied to words and conduct, and so moved towards its 'ordinary modern meaning', as defined below.) As a synonym for 'amable', its career ran, in the examples given, from 1535 to 1788. (And it is here, one may add, that Johnson's emphasis falls.) Having distinguished these two archaic senses, *The Oxford English Dictionary* continues: 'The ordinary modern meaning mixes senses 1 and 2, implying the possession of that friendly disposition which causes one to be liked; habitually characterized by that friendliness which awakens friendliness in return; having pleasing qualities of heart.' The first recorded example of this usage comes from *Tom Jones* (1749); but it is followed by a better one, from the first volume (1776) of Gibbon: 'That amiable prince soon acquired the affections of the public.'

But is it necessary so formally to approach a word commonly used in Jane Austen's time—and freely used in Highbury's idlest conversations? Isabella has long known the "'sweet, amiable Jane Fairfax'" (104); but, at a time when she makes no doubt that Frank Churchill is "'a most amiable young man'" (96), she has never even met him. In using the word of Dixon (160), Miss Campbell (161), and even Mrs Elton (285), Miss Bates is still less discriminating. And the narrator sarcastically records that, long before Miss Hawkins arrived in Highbury, "she was, by some means or other, discovered to have every recommendation of person and mind; to be handsome, elegant, highly accomplished, and perfectly amiable" (181). Against this background, the objection might run, it would be surprising if Emma did *not* call Frank Churchill "amiable"; and the concurrence of an ambiguity in Emma's attitude to that disingenuous young man with a word that happens to have an ambiguous history might be regarded as an accident.

But the weight of evidence requires that this objection be dismissed. In the first place, Emma has little patience with the "nothing-meaning terms" (270) of polite conversation. When she has induced Miss Bates to admit that, compared to her niece, "'Miss Campbell always was absolutely plain—but extremely elegant and amiable'", Emma comments drily on the proviso, "'Yes, that of course'" (161). The inference that Emma herself would use the word more carefully finds wide support. At first she misapplies it, as naturally she must. When she busily recommends Harriet to Elton (43) and Elton to Harriet (75) as being "'amiable'", her misuse of the word reflects her misunderstanding of the situation. Upon discovering the truth, Emma consoles herself by arguing that Mr Elton's very presumptuousness shows that he is not "so particularly amiable as to make it shocking to disappoint him" (138). There is no such consolation in the thought that "all that was amiable . . . seemed on Harriet's side, not her own" (141). Her new opinions prove more accurate. When Elton snubs Harriet at the ball, Emma bitterly recalls that "This was Mr. Elton! the amiable, obliging, gentle Mr. Elton" (328). And even Mr Knightley will call Harriet "'an artless, amiable girl'" (474).

Emma first suggests that Frank Churchill may be "'an amiable young man'" (148) when she and Mr Knightley quarrel so bitterly about him. Mr Knightley replies that "'your amiable young man is a very weak young man, if this be the first occasion of his carrying

through a resolution to do right against the will of others'" (148).
A little later in the quarrel, he grows even more emphatic:

"No, Emma, your amiable young man can be amiable only in French, not in English. He may be very 'aimable,' have very good manners, and be very agreeable; but he can have no English delicacy towards the feelings o other people: nothing really amiable about him." (149)

Grounded as it is on the evidence of Frank Churchill's letters and of Mrs Weston's uncertainties, this important distinction represents Mr Knightley's then opinion of Frank Churchill at its least speculative and most penetrating. And yet he does more justice to the young man than to Emma's word for him. *His* distinction between "amiable" and "aimable" quite excludes those connotations of love which are the essence of Johnson's definition and which—as in our other examples—impinge on Jane Austen's usage. The inference that Mr Knightley is afraid of what Emma's "amiable" may imply is supported by the injured tone of his repeated phrase, "*your* amiable young man". But Emma promptly rejects Mr Knightley's distinction and clings the more strongly to her word and her opinion.

When she meets Frank Churchill, Emma is struck at first by the disparity between the "amiable" (191) feelings that he professes towards Highbury and his long delay in coming there. By the next morning, however, she is persuaded that these "very amiable feelings" (197) are perfectly genuine; "that he had not been acting a part, or making a parade of insincere professions; and that Mr. Knightley certainly had not done him justice" (197). These comments are soon followed by the Coles' dinner-party, where Emma's confidence in Frank Churchill reaches its zenith and begins to fall away. We have seen that, even after the decline of their intimacy, Emma's fantasy of love continues; and it is in this sense—an ironically diminished sense—that she calls him "amiable" for the last time:

Had she intended ever to *marry* him, it might have been worth while to pause and consider, and try to understand the value of his preference, and the character of his temper; but for all the purposes of their acquaintance, he was quite amiable enough. (250)

On learning the truth about Elton, Emma simply reverses her opinion: he had seemed amiable; he now proves otherwise. But, when Frank Churchill betrays her trust, she drops both man and word. Never again does she use "amiable" in any favourable sense. In its new, harsh sense, it appears for the first time in the preceding chapter: "This amiable, upright, perfect Jane Fairfax was apparently cherishing very reprehensible feelings" (243). She uses it as

95

bitterly, in a passage already quoted, when Elton snubs Harriet at the ball (328). And she will apply it to herself in tones ranging from wry self-mockery (450) to the more serious reproach of "'one of my amiable fits, about ten years ago. I did it because I thought it would offend you'" (462-3).

When this striking change in Emma's usage is set beside Elton's devious praise for the "fair, lovely, amiable" (124) Miss Smith and Frank Churchill's doubtful praise for the "'amiable and delightful'"(438) Miss Woodhouse, it might appear that Jane Austen regards the word as unfit for honest use. But this is not so. The narrator uses it, simply and seriously, of both John (139) and Isabella (92) Knightley. And so, again, when Mr Knightley goes to Brunswick Square "to learn to be indifferent" to Emma: "he had gone to a wrong place. There was too much domestic happiness in his brother's house; woman wore too amiable a form in it" (432-3). It seems unlikely that Jane Austen consciously chose to manage this word—or others, like "elegant" and "agreeable"—in the complicated way I have described. But, whether or not she made of it a conscious motif, its course through the novel shows how exactly she expresses her meaning and how thoroughly she understands her characters in all their shifts of mood.

VI

When Frank Churchill leaves Highbury, some forty pages of the second volume remain. In those pages, Emma's attachment to Mr Knightley, still unrecognized by her, expresses itself more plainly than before. She relies on him increasingly as her criterion of the masculine virtues and, when she is considering what her friends will think of Mrs Elton, her mind runs first to him. Such is her ability to deceive herself, however, that when Frank Churchill eventually comes to mind, she stops short and "glibly" (279) comments, "'Ah! there I am—thinking of him directly. Always the first person to be thought of! How I catch myself out!'" (279). Soon after this she nerves herself finally to settle the question of Mr Knightley's opinion of Jane Fairfax. But neither the urgency of her question nor the relief afforded by his answer can teach her why she had to ask.

Meanwhile Mr Knightley gains less than he might have hoped from the departure of his rival. Emma's apparent willingness to contemplate a match between Jane Fairfax and himself can only mean that Frank Churchill stands first in her own plans—reason enough for Mr Knightley to grow "thoughtful" and to speak "in a manner which shewed him not pleased" (287). Even in an innocent conversation about hand-writing, when he is thinking with pleasure of Emma's striking hand, she must introduce the fellow's name. Undaunted by a terse comment on writing that is "'like a woman's'" (297), she speaks of having a convincing specimen in her writing-desk; and, worst of all, Mrs Weston seems to imply that it was decidedly a *billet-doux*. Like Mr Woodhouse, then, he is not "particularly delighted" (304) when Weston brings the glad tidings of his son's return. And he declares that, if the renewal of Emma's social activities takes her from her little nephews, they can always "'be sent to Donwell. I shall certainly be at leisure'" (312).

Poor Mr Knightley! If he could only know it, his rival's cause— such as it was—is already lost. For Emma has other plans for Frank Churchill. Such "'tenderness of heart'" (269) as Harriet's, so gratifyingly expressed in recent compliments, must not go un- rewarded. Transcending as it so obviously does the clearer heads, longer sight, and better judgement of women like Jane Fairfax and herself, it is the very quality that marriage requires: "'for a wife— a sensible man's wife—it is invaluable. I mention no names; but happy the man who changes Emma for Harriet!'" (269). The mag- nificent dramatic irony of this passage lies partly in the way those most concerned remain unimpressed by Harriet's remarkable tenderness of heart; and there is the associated development of that recurrent phrase, "a sensible man". Though Frank Churchill is the sensible man whom Emma has in mind, we do well to remember that both Robert Martin and Mr Knightley have an older and more reasonable claim to the title.

But the weight of these forty pages falls on Elton's bride. Her first words are of "'my brother Mr. Suckling's seat'" (272); and though the recency of his purchase is not yet established, the use of "seat" is ominous. The resemblances she is pleased to detect between Hartfield and Maple Grove are so utterly unremarkable that she can only be parading the Suckling alliance. And even her belief that Surrey alone is "'the garden of England'" (273) reveals her wish to shine. Having been "'transplanted'" (273) from Maple Grove, her inimitable bloom requires the most beauteous of settings.

Her wish to shine is also evident in what Miss Lascelles calls her 'general and insidious misuse of language in the interests of an ugly smartness'.[15] This is to be seen at its simplest in such affected elegancies as *caro sposo*;[16] in such trite poeticisms as "'Hymen's

15. Mary Lascelles, *Jane Austen and Her Art*, p. 114.
16. In a note on p. 278, Dr Chapman records that the edition of 1816, the sole authoritative text, gives: *cara sposo* (278, 279); *cara sposa* (302); and *caro sposo* (356). Apparently he has sought—without complete success—to normalize throughout. But 1816 may represent Jane Austen's intention: Mrs Elton's uncertain variations are what might be expected; and, in using a false form, Emma may be mocking her.

saffron robe'" (308); in such modish phrases as "'in the first circle'";[17] in such failures of comprehension as "'*mediocre* to the last degree'" (276); and in such absurd pomposities as her use of "'exploring'" (274, 354) for a journey where even the ladies might very well have walked.[18]

Beyond these tortured phrases lies that genius for hollow but estimable sentiments which first appears in the soulful declaration that, after "'many happy months'", Maple Grove seemed "'quite a home'" (273). It appears again when she, who had conditioned only for a musical society, must sacrifice her art to the labours of domesticity: her housekeeper alone needs her for half an hour a day. Like her extortion of compliments (302, 307) and her espousal of the cause of injured femininity (305), her concern for her prerogatives as a bride further testifies to her craving for admiration. But even here she is betrayed into absurdity by the extravagance of her demands. Not content with Mr Woodhouse's marked attentions, she must flatter herself that, solely on her account, "'this dear old beau of mine'" (302) has left the table before the other men. She could not know that this is his unfailing custom (cf. 122): but anyone else would allow for the existence of motives not personally addressed.

Only when Mrs Elton is with her 'inferiors', however, does she really come into her own. The "'sweet, interesting'" (282) Jane Fairfax must be brought forward, whether she likes it or not. Her reserve is only timidity: and timidity, "'in those who are at all inferior, . . . is extremely prepossessing'" (283). A situation must be found for her—in the first circle, of course. In the meantime, there need be no difficulty about feeding her as we are accustomed to a lavish way of living. Her letters can be collected by "'one of our men, I forget his name'" (295). She can be given an occasional airing in one or another of our carriages. And, if we do not always

17. Mrs Elton often speaks (e.g. 300, 301) of positions "in the first circle" of society. And Emma's mocking reference to "first circles, spheres, lines, ranks, every thing" (359) is echoed in 'Sanditon': ". . . the Miss Beauforts were soon satisfied with 'the Circle in which they moved in Sanditon' to use a proper phrase, for every body must now 'move in a Circle',—to the prevalence of which rototory Motion, is perhaps to be attributed the Giddiness & false steps of many" (*Minor Works*, p. 422).

18. Her advice to Anna Austen (*Letters*, p. 394) shows that Jane Austen would have tried to be accurate about distances. Now 'Maple Grove' is 125 miles from London (306), in the vicinity of Bristol. Since a contemporary road-book places Bristol 119¾ miles from London, with King's Weston 5¼ miles further on, 'Maple Grove' and King's Weston might almost adjoin each other. *See* D. Paterson, *A New and Accurate Description of the Direct and Principal Cross Roads in England and Wales*, 15th edn, London 1811, p. 87.

remember our promises to call for her (320-1), why, then, it is scarcely her place to complain.

Although Emma had resolved not to judge Mr Elton's bride too hastily, her ill-opinion is not long delayed. It is of particular interest because there is a glimpse or two of herself in her description of Mrs Elton as having drawn:

... all her notions ... from one set of people, and one style of living; that if not foolish she was ignorant, and that her society would certainly do Mr. Elton no good.
Harriet would have been a better match. If not wise or refined herself, she would have connected him with those who were... (272)

The magnificent self-importance of this last sentence echoes an earlier argument for admiring Harriet (62) and effectively cuts away *her* reason for believing Harriet the better match. And we have long since grown familiar with the effects of Emma's drawing all her notions "from one set of people, and one style of living". It must be added that Mrs Elton's assiduous pride in her "resources" (276, 277, 290, 307, 356) and her desire to seem "gracious" (305, 321, 453, 455) have both been pre-empted by Emma (85; 22, 53, 260); that Mrs Elton and Emma will contend for Highbury's throne; and that Mrs Elton's bullying of Jane Fairfax faintly resembles Emma's exploitation of the willing Harriet. Swept off their feet by such points of resemblance, some modern critics have actually regarded Mrs Elton as a second Emma.[19]

But surely Mrs Elton's leading function, by virtue of which she transcends Jane Austen's earlier caricatures of selfishness, is to be contrasted with the heroine. Like all good contrasts, it is grounded in an initial area of resemblance. And, as Emma advances towards womanhood, the contrast grows more and more extreme.

From the very first, however, there is one difference so important that, except in the gloomy climate of much modern criticism, it could never be obscured. Whereas Mrs Elton is absorbed forever in her dreary self-parade, Emma can laugh—and laugh at herself. Even when she is laughing at others, one can make no worse objection than Mrs Weston: "'For shame, Emma! Do not mimic her. You divert me against my conscience'" (225). When Frank Churchill comes despondently to Donwell Abbey, thinking of his quarrel with Jane Fairfax but talking only of the heat, the sparkling play of Emma's wit soon cools him and revives him. When Mr Knightley grows pompous about Frank Churchill's filial duty, Emma laughs him out of court with her picture of how the young

19. Marvin Mudrick, *Jane Austen: Irony as Defense and Discovery*, p. 194.

man would address his step-mother, "'standing up in the middle of the room, I suppose, and speaking as loud as he could!'" (147). And, when she turns her wit against herself, she is more irresistible than ever. Thus, when Mrs Weston suddenly discovers "that Mrs. Elton must be asked to begin the ball", Emma hears "the sad truth with fortitude" and wryly decides it is "almost enough to make her think of marrying" (325). To Mr Knightley's remark that, instead of scolding her, he will leave her to her own reflections, she replies, "'Can you trust me with such flatterers?'" (330). And again, when Mr Knightley asks in mock indignation, "'What do you deserve?'", she replies, "'Oh! I always deserve the best treatment, because I never put up with any other'" (474). As Bradley said of those who think that Elizabeth Bennet married Pemberley, 'But what is the use of my quoting this? Anyone capable of seriously making the charge will take this for a confession of its truth.'[20]

The second volume ends with a conversation which bears on our recent argument and which—like that argument—points forward to the future. John Knightley tells Emma, "'Your neighbourhood is increasing, and you mix more with it'" (311-12). His brother dourly comments, with Frank Churchill in mind, that "'Randalls . . . does it all'" (312). Emma laughingly points out John Knightley's motive for saying so and expresses herself puzzled that his brother should agree. After all, her "'amazing engagements'" have amounted to "'dining once with the Coles—and having a ball talked of, which never took place'" (312). Although the literal truth is on Emma's side, the second volume has been chiefly given over to the increase of Emma's neighbourhood. She has often, if tacitly, acceded to her father's sole criterion of friendship, the subject of a dozen of his absurd *non sequiturs*, the question of whether he has known a person for a sufficient number of years. For Emma, though never for her father, that criterion has come under increasing pressure throughout the second volume. In the third volume, it is finally to be overthrown: not by the influence of still further new arrivals but by Emma's discovering that, even among the people she claims to know, there are many—herself not least among them —whom she scarcely knows at all.

20. A. C. Bradley, 'Jane Austen', *Essays and Studies*, Vol. ii (1911), p. 32n.

CHAPTER III

Volume Three

I

The earlier part of the third volume is marked by 'social' episodes like those that occupy the middle stages of the novel. But, after this brilliant series culminates at Box Hill, Jane Austen suddenly narrows her focus. Most critics of *Emma* write as if the remainder of the novel —which occupies over a hundred pages—amounted only to a proposal and an acceptance. Yet it is here that Jane Austen shows Emma and Mr Knightley patiently resolving their old differences. It is here that she sets most of the earlier action in a new perspective. And it is here, in a final series of quiet but deeply thoughtful conversations, that she secures the love between them and shows that it will prosper.

These particular possibilities seem remote when the volume opens upon a chapter in which the narrator, speaking for Emma, fore-shadows "a crisis, an event, a something to alter her present composed and tranquil state" (315). On taking stock of her feelings about Frank Churchill's return, Emma finds that she is concerned only lest his affection may prove embarrassing. She is soon re-assured on this point but remains puzzled by his restless manner. Meanwhile he and the Westons continue as before, he manufacturing excuses for calling on Jane Fairfax, they persuading themselves that he and Emma grow ever more attached. The future is also served when Frank Churchill is brought to Richmond, only nine miles from Highbury, and when Mrs Churchill's failing health is empha-sized. Compared with some other episodes nearby, this whole chapter is prosaic: it is as if a mountaineer were securing his forward-camp before striking out for the summit.

The advance begins with the ball at the Crown Inn. Miss Bates is never more valuable than in this episode. By virtue of her incessant talk of everything about her, she becomes an unofficial assistant to the narrator. At times her remarks are unwittingly revealing, as when she lets us see Mrs Elton's relentless desire to be " 'the queen of the evening' " (329); when her unavailing attempts to catch Jane

Fairfax's attention imply that Jane Fairfax's attention is firmly fixed elsewhere; or when she speaks gratefully of Frank Churchill's many little courtesies and tells him how often they talk of him among themselves. And yet there is a sense in which her idlest chatter is no less important. Through her we learn of the Hughes family and the Otways; of the matting in the passage and the lighting in the hall; of her being served soup and her mother's being denied the Hartfield asparagus. Through her, in short, the ball grows real as we read of it. And, because she is so willing to chronicle small beer, the narrator proper is left free to comment more coolly and intelligently.

There is one event which even "Emma thought something of" (326), and one or two others which matter more than she knows. Ever since the Christmas party at Randalls, there has been an increasing disparity between the narrator's comments on Mr Weston and Emma's unabated esteem. Emma, who must learn to distinguish justly between Mr Weston's promiscuous agreeableness and the less yielding attitudes of Mr Knightley, takes a step forward on the evening of the ball. A little offended that Mr Weston has particularly asked so many others to come early, she rises to an important distinction between "general benevolence" and "general friendship" (320); and she feels she can imagine a man whose behaviour would be governed by the one without his being too lavish of the other. This is scarcely the Emma who had allowed Mr Elton's agreeableness the advantage over "'Mr. Knightley's downright, decided, commanding sort of manner'" (34) or who, on the evening of the snow, had taken as little notice of Mr Knightley's thoughtfulness as of Mr Weston's heartless sociability. It is the last time, moreover, that she allows even an implicit comparison between Mr Knightley and these others. Weston is soon to lump everyone together for the excursion to Box Hill. For his wife's sake, Emma says nothing of his casually flouting so many known animosities; but "the forbearance of her outward submission left a heavy arrear due of secret severity in her reflections on the unmanageable good-will of Mr. Weston's temper" (353). Although Emma's anger soon passes, he never regains her respect. By the end of the novel, indeed, she is accepting his indiscretions with all the good-humoured resignation of his wife. And, having seen how little he respects Mr Churchill's reasonable desire to keep one engagement secret for a few weeks, Emma and Mr Knightley choose him to spread the secret of their own. They are not disappointed.

Another incident of more importance than Emma is aware occurs after she overhears Mrs Elton, who has just been introduced to

Frank Churchill, growing loud in praise for him. Emma tells him that he is ungrateful to dislike such a person and is astonished when he rounds on *her*. But, being interrupted at that moment by Mrs Weston, she goes no further than to suppose that he is "in an odd humour" (325). He imagines, of course, that she is referring to Mrs Elton's patronage of Jane Fairfax, which he has never actually seen before; and he concludes, not for the first time, that, guessing his secret, Emma is heartlessly mocking him.

Emma passes over Mrs Elton's treatment of Jane Fairfax not because she condones it but because she has no reason to suppose that it would interest Frank Churchill. For, at a time when Mr Knightley's faith in human reason and human decency had extended even to Mrs Elton, Emma had shown a much keener sense of the realities. Arguing as usual from the universal operation of sound principles, Mr Knightley had held that Mrs Elton would never speak to Miss Fairfax as she spoke of her:

". . . you may be sure that Miss Fairfax awes Mrs. Elton by her superiority both of mind and manner; and that face to face Mrs. Elton treats her with all the respect which she has a claim to. Such a woman as Jane Fairfax probably never fell in Mrs. Elton's way before—and no degree of vanity can prevent her acknowledging her own comparative littleness in action, if not in consciousness." (286-7)

After first settling a more urgent question, Emma had joined issue:

"I can much more readily enter into the temptation of getting away from Miss Bates, than I can believe in the triumph of Miss Fairfax's mind over Mrs. Elton. I have no faith in Mrs. Elton's acknowledging herself the inferior in thought, word, or deed; or in her being under any restraint beyond her own scanty rule of good-breeding." (288)

Even that scanty rule is forgotten in the incident of which Emma does take note. For, when Elton so ostentatiously leaves Harriet without a partner, Emma "perceived that his wife, who was standing immediately above her, was not only listening also, but even encouraging him by significant glances" (327). Emma is probably right in thinking Elton not "quite so hardened as his wife, though growing very like her" (328); and Mr Knightley is quite right in thinking that "'they aimed at wounding more than Harriet'" (330). But, for us at least, the main interest lies in following the effects now set in motion. Harriet loses one hero only to find another. Having rescued her, Mr Knightley has actually to talk with her. And Emma is "all pleasure and gratitude, both for Harriet and herself" (328).

Mr Knightley has been much in her mind that evening. Noticing him "among the standers-by, where he ought not to be" (325), she is struck for the first time by his physical presence: by his youthful looks; by his "tall, firm, upright figure, among the bulky forms and stooping shoulders of the elderly men" (326); and by the natural grace of his movements. This potent insight is robbed of immediate effect by her ever-present fear that he watches her only to criticize.

At supper afterwards, Emma still cannot bring herself to confess the whole sorry story of the Elton affair: but she freely admits that Mr Knightley's judgement had been superior to her own. And, though his manner remains a little heavy, Mr Knightley is happy to reciprocate:

". . . in return for your acknowledging so much, I will do you the justice to say, that you would have chosen for him better than he has chosen for himself.—Harriet Smith has some first-rate qualities, which Mrs. Elton is totally without. An unpretending, single-minded, artless girl—infinitely to be preferred by any man of sense and taste to such a woman as Mrs. Elton. I found Harriet more conversable than I expected." (331)

His new estimate of Harriet, with its reference to "any man of sense and taste", is to trouble Emma later. But, for the present, they are as happy together as they have ever been. With a delightful mixture, on both sides, of eagerness and diffidence, they agree to dance together. Her reference to his dancing and to their being not *too* much brother and sister—itself a change from father and daughter—shows that her new sense of his physical presence is still awake. And his reply shows that he is a long step ahead: "'Brother and sister! no, indeed'" (331).

On the following morning, while Emma is still thinking happily of these events and looking forward complacently to a summer with "Harriet rational, Frank Churchill not too much in love, and Mr. Knightley not wanting to quarrel with her" (332), new misunderstandings are being set in train. For Harriet is even then suffering her second misadventure and being rescued for a second time. The essential point here is not that Emma misjudges the relative importance of the two incidents but that, without even remembering that there have been two incidents, she fits the adventure of the gypsies into her pre-conceived scheme that Frank Churchill and Harriet should marry. In a quiet place like Highbury, the incident itself is remarkable; and "knowing, as she did, the favourable state of mind of each at this period, it struck her the more. He was wishing to get the better of his attachment to herself, she just recovering from her mania for Mr. Elton" (335).

Amidst a welter of imputed motives and groundless claims to knowledge, this last clause is Emma's only point of contact with reality. Beyond this, she is too busy in congratulating herself on having predicted their attachment and in allowing her fancy to run riot. There are warning signs like her self-satisfied claim, in a famous passage, that she is an "imaginist" (335); her trite phrases about what happened "to the very person, and at the very hour, when the other very person was chancing to pass by to rescue her" (335); and her disguising the actual Harriet and the actual Frank Churchill from herself by swathing them in the conventional garb of "a fine young man and a lovely young woman thrown together in such a way" (334). Given Harriet's loose use of words, Emma can be forgiven for not seeing that her feeling of "'veneration'" (341) for her unnamed rescuer and her memory of his "'noble look'" (342) sit none too comfortably on Frank Churchill. But she might have listened more carefully to *his* story. His comment on Harriet's "'naïveté'" (335), for example, is hardly that of a lover. Worse still, it is the very word he had used of Harriet after their first meeting (220). And, worst of all, it had been Elton's word for Miss Woodhouse's little friend (48).

Evidently her experience with Elton has taught Emma less than it might. But, by restraining her from speaking openly without teaching her how to preserve a perfect silence, even the lesson she did learn is to work to her disadvantage. Despite the hopes she builds on Harriet's adventure, Emma resolves neither to "stir a step, nor drop a hint" (335). This resolution is severely tested when Harriet unexpectedly declares that she will never marry. "After a moment's debate, as to whether it should pass unnoticed" (341), Emma adroitly inquires if she is still thinking of Mr Elton. Harriet indignantly repudiates this notion and stammers something about someone far superior. Utterly determined against any return to their old unreserve, their "open and frequent discussion of hopes and chances" (341), Emma is inclined to go no further. But, knowing that complete silence will make too radical a departure from their former habit, that it will either offend Harriet or produce unwanted confidences, Emma feels obliged to say a little more. That little is too much. For there follows a restrained and ambiguous conversation which does nothing to correct Emma's idea that Harriet loves Frank Churchill, which raises Harriet's hopes of winning Mr Knightley, and which effectively prevents them from entering on the subject again.

The following chapter opens with an account of Highbury in early June, an account that includes a last instance of the disingenuous narration we have previously discussed: "Mr. Knightley, who, *for some reason best known to himself*, had certainly taken an early dislike to Frank Churchill . . ." (343; my italics). Only a few lines later, such part-truths cease finally to be required. For Mr Knightley begins to suspect Frank Churchill's actual motives; the narrator is immediately relieved of a growing burden of credibility; and, though the whole truth has yet to be discovered, the reader no longer dwells in Emma's ignorance.

Mr Knightley has been deceived until now by a seemingly impressive body of evidence, by Frank Churchill's "own attentions [to Emma], his father's hints, his mother-in-law's guarded silence; it was all in unison; words, conduct, discretion, and indiscretion, told the same story" (343). Against all this he has nothing to set at first but "a look, more than a single look, at Miss Fairfax, which, from the admirer of Miss Woodhouse, seemed somewhat out of place" (343-4). By quoting Cowper against himself, he resists such over-confidence as Emma's and also supplies, in effect, a motto for the novel: "'Myself creating what I saw'" (344). He resolves, nevertheless, to watch the more.

When everyone meets near Hartfield one afternoon and Frank Churchill makes his celebrated blunder about Perry's carriage, the conversation runs wide but true. Frank Churchill recovers quickly enough to talk distractingly about dreams and to find amusement in what follows; Jane Fairfax resolutely refuses to be drawn; Weston begins by taking up the gossip about Perry and ends by dropping hints to Emma about dreaming; and Miss Bates declares that she must speak—of Jane's discretion. Mr Knightley says nothing but notices everything. He still watches silently throughout the word-game, with its "blunder", its "Dixon", and—if only in the Austens' family tradition—its abortive plea for "pardon"; with its "sly and demure" looks from Frank Churchill; with the "eager laughing warmth" (348) of Emma's intervention; and with Jane Fairfax's mounting annoyance and abrupt departure.

He remained at Hartfield after all the rest, his thoughts full of what he had seen; so full, that when the candles came to assist his observations, he must—yes, he certainly must, as a friend—an anxious friend—give Emma some hint, ask her some question. He could not see her in a situation of such danger, without trying to preserve her. It was his duty. (349)

He cautiously asks Emma the point of the word that had so entertained her and distressed Miss Fairfax. When she will say no more than that "'it all meant nothing; a mere joke among ourselves'", he stops to think again:

A variety of evils crossed his mind. Interference—fruitless interference. Emma's confusion, and the acknowledged intimacy, seemed to declare her affection engaged. Yet he would speak. He owed it to her, to risk any thing that might be involved in an unwelcome interference, rather than her welfare; to encounter any thing, rather than the remembrance of neglect in such a cause. (350)

These two passages of reflection show Mr Knightley at his best. On the one hand, as always, he knows his duty and abides by it. The broken rhythms, the doubts and irresolutions, of the first passage are only as to the means he might employ: and they are swept away by the simple finality of "it was his duty". On the other hand, he recognizes, as never before, that Emma is an individual in her own right, his protégée no longer. He acknow-ledges now, as he will later acknowledge to her (462), the evils of interference. He respects her embarrassment. He cannot but believe that she loves Frank Churchill. But, whatever the cost to himself, her welfare must come first. He can endure anything but the future "remembrance of neglect in such a cause". So, once again, he takes up his burden: "Yet he would speak." No doubt his manner is still fatherly; but the old complacent paternalism has gone and will return no more.[1]

Meanwhile his seriousness is tempered for us by Jane Austen's searching wit. Mr Knightley will speak to Emma not as a father, not as a brother—and certainly not as a disappointed lover. He will speak, so *he* believes, "as a friend—an anxious friend". So success-fully does the word disguise his real motive from himself that—like Emma with her "little Henry"—he will rely on it again. It is as a "friend" (375) that he rebukes Emma at Box Hill. And, in a wonderful reversal, it is " 'as a friend' " (429) that Emma urges him to confess what she supposes is his love for Harriet:

"As a friend!"—repeated Mr. Knightley.—"Emma, that I fear is a word —No, I have no wish—Stay, yes, why should I hesitate?—I have gone too far already for concealment.—Emma, I accept your offer—Extraordinary as it may seem, I accept it, and refer myself to you as a friend.—Tell me, then, have I no chance of ever succeeding?" (429-30)

But we must revert to the first of these gestures of "friendship". Knowing that Emma will vouchsafe no further answer to his question about the word-game, he approaches more directly. Emma, of course, is astonished by the very idea that Frank Churchill and Jane Fairfax may be attached. At first she is content to deny the suggestion "with a most open eagerness" (350). But, when Mr Knightley is so rash as to speak of what he has been *imagining*, Emma's amusement knows no bounds. Unfortunately for

1. Mr Robert Liddell illustrates Jane Austen's habit of naming characters after members of her family: *The Novels of Jane Austen*, pp. 95-7. One may add to the list: for Mr Knightley bears her father's Christian name.

both of them, her extravagant manner confirms his gravest fears. Even when, in a moment of seriousness, she allows a distinction between things she presumes and things she can—so she believes— positively answer for, she only distresses him the more:

". . . they are as far from any attachment or admiration for one another, as any two beings in the world can be. That is, I *presume* it to be so on her side, and I can *answer* for its being so on his. I will answer for the gentleman's indifference."

She spoke with a confidence which staggered, with a satisfaction which silenced, Mr. Knightley. (351)

After being drawn into it almost by accident, Mr Knightley seems to regard the strawberry-party a few days later as a gesture of farewell to Emma. In inviting Mr Woodhouse, he lifts the party quite out of the ranks of more ordinary events. In discreetly attempting to exclude Frank Churchill, he seems to want Emma to himself, perhaps for the last time. In stepping forward as Harriet's friend and protector, he assumes a responsibility that Emma must soon relinquish. Even his declaration that, until there is a Mrs Knightley of Donwell, he must manage its entertaining for himself has the wryly philosophic air of one who, without recovering his contentment, has regained his self-command.

On the day itself, even Miss Bates is silenced so that Emma can keep our attention: for this is the last occasion on which she keeps the freedom of her old fool's paradise. All around her there are signs of the mounting tension that is to explode next day at Box Hill. Yet she passes the pleasantest of mornings, refreshing her memory of the Abbey and feeling "all the honest pride and complacency which her alliance with the present and future proprietor could fairly warrant" (358). No doubt there is an element of the proprietary in this complacency. No doubt she is also rationalizing a more personal interest in a place which so perfectly reflects Mr Knightley's tastes and attitudes. Yet simultaneously— and quite in defiance of fashionable taste—she feels a simple, spontaneous delight in everything she sees: in the rambling, comfortable old house; in its pleasant grounds; and, despite a prick of memory, in a vista of meadows, river, woods—and the Abbey Mill Farm.

There is an equally delicate balance in Emma's treatment of her fellows that morning. As we have seen, she is much to blame for being so ignorant of their actual joys and sorrows. Yet, within the limits of her knowledge, she acts for the best. She knows nothing of Mr Knightley's anxiety for her or his personal unhappiness: but she responds kindly and thoughtfully to Mrs Weston's growing concern for Frank's lateness, her fear of his black mare. She knows nothing of Harriet's dreams of Mr Knightley: but she is relieved to see that Harriet's 'anxiety' about Frank Churchill is being held in check. She does not know the full extent of Jane Fairfax's distress: but she sympathetically accedes to Jane's heartfelt pleas for solitude. She does not know that, when Frank Churchill arrives at last, he has been quarrelling with Jane Fairfax: but she humours him until he recovers his spirits. Unfortunately for Emma, the only reward of her morning's work is that Frank Churchill is encouraged to stay overnight at Randalls, and go with them to Box Hill.

He is later to write of his quarrel with Jane Fairfax. She had never approved of his use of Emma as a shield for his intentions; and, with what he learns to think "'a very natural and consistent degree of discretion'", had refused his offer to escort her back to Highbury: "'While I, to blind the world to our engagement, was behaving one hour with objectionable particularity to another woman, was she to be consenting the next to a proposal which might have made every previous caution useless?'" (441). At the time, however, he regards her caution as a mark of coldness and doubts her affection. The next day at Box Hill, he behaves with "'such shameful, insolent neglect of her, and such apparent devotion to Miss W., as it would have been impossible for any woman of sense to endure'" (441). (It is not merely that he flirts with Emma. His particular gallantries are designed to imply that he and Emma have long been in collusion; and the replies they evoke from Emma point, all unwittingly, to the same thing.) Jane Fairfax, in turn, is led to speak "'her resentment in a form of words perfectly intelligible to me'" (441); to regard their engagement as at an end; and, upon learning of his angry departure for Richmond that evening, to accept Mrs Smallridge's delightful situation.

Emma, as usual, is sensitive to the moods of others while ignorant of their motives. For a time after their arrival, "it was downright dulness to Emma. She had never seen Frank Churchill so silent and stupid. . . . While he was so dull, it was no wonder that Harriet should be dull likewise, and they were both insufferable" (367). But, when he grows "talkative and gay, making her his first object" (367-8), she is quick to respond. "Not that Emma was gay and thoughtless from any real felicity; it was rather because she felt less happy than she had expected. She laughed because she was disappointed" (368). He seems, in short, to offer a diversion. She knows that it all means nothing; and, if the onlookers should think of them as flirting excessively, so much the more diverting.

With Frank Churchill playing one game and Emma playing another, their exchanges take on the brilliance, the hardness, and the artificiality of Congreve *en pastiche*.[2] How swiftly they catch up each other's words. How adroitly they mimic the time-worn language of haughty mistress and perpetual thrall. How suitably Frank Churchill lets his "accents swell", his chorus of "February" sound and sound again:

"I am perfectly comfortable to-day."
"You are comfortable because you are under command."
"Your command?—Yes."
"Perhaps I intended you to say so, but I meant self-command." . . .

"You order me, whether you speak or not. And you can be always with me. You are always with me."
"Dating from three o'clock yesterday. My perpetual influence could not begin earlier, or you would not have been so much out of humour before."
"Three o'clock yesterday! That is your date. I thought I had seen you first in February." . . .

"I saw you first in February. Let every body on the Hill hear me if they can. Let my accents swell to Mickleham on one side, and Dorking on the other. I saw you first in February." (368-9)

Less easy than he about "'talking nonsense for the entertainment of seven silent people'", Emma is positively self-conscious about his announcement that "'Miss Woodhouse (who, wherever she is, presides,) . . . desires to know what you are all thinking of.'" And, when Mr Knightley asks if she would really like to know what they are thinking, she answers, "laughing as carelessly as she could" (369), that it is the very last thing she would "'stand the brunt of just now'" (370). Yet, as so often, Mr Knightley's attempt to check her leads only to new exaggerations. Frank Churchill grows ever more ingenious. The Eltons' aggrieved mutterings, especially on the touchy subject of acrostics, are just those of any Mar-wits. And so the play goes on.

The clown's part is filled when poor Miss Bates blunders out of the wings, confessing her own dullness and "looking round with the most good-humoured dependence on every body's assent". Emma, we are told, "could not resist". Conceding her the requisite "ma'am" —a form of address she does not ordinarily use—she polishes her off with epigrammatic ease: "'Ah! ma'am, but there may be a difficulty. Pardon me—but you will be limited as to number—only three at once'" (370). Miss Bates seems to forget that she is only in a play and seeks comfort from Mr Knightley. But, after only a moment's pause, the merriment continues. Mr Weston produces his little conundrum about Emma's unmistakable perfection. Mr

2. After writing of the Box Hill episode, I found that Professor Richard Poirier approaches it along rather similar lines: *A World Elsewhere*, pp. 163-75.

Knightley crowns the joke with a truer and more searching wit. The Eltons, unable to lead, decide not to compete. The party dwindles. And eventually Frank Churchill is to be heard in soliloquy, his spirits still rising "to a pitch almost unpleasant. Even Emma grew tired at last of flattery and merriment, and wished herself rather walking quietly about with any of the others" (374).

Emma has tired at last of a dramatic fairyland—like that pictured in Lamb's well-known essay—where wit flourishes without hindrance or compunction, where there is neither right nor wrong. But Lamb says that the fairyland would vanish at the touch of a single 'good character, a single gush of moral feeling, a revulsion of the judgment to actual life and actual duties'.[3] At Box Hill, the revulsion occurs, at least for us, when Miss Bates stammers, "'Ah!—well—to be sure. Yes, I see what she means, (turning to Mr. Knightley,) and I will try to hold my tongue. I must make myself very disagreeable, or she would not have said such a thing to an old friend'" (371).

For Emma, however, there is no full awakening until Mr Knightley rebukes her. She has spoken not with real malice but, as he says, "'in thoughtless spirits, and the pride of the moment'" (375). Yet the action alone is enough when it is directed at a woman of Miss Bates' "'character, age, and situation'" (374) and when it is performed "'before others, many of whom (certainly *some*,) would be entirely guided by *your* treatment of her'" (375). Although Mr Knightley is deceived by Emma's first, instinctive rejection of these charges and, a moment later, by her keeping "her face averted, and her tongue motionless" (375), his reprimand does sink home, as never before, because 'it awakens part of herself, and comes as the voice of her own conscience'.[4] Her real feelings are "only of anger against herself, mortification, and deep concern" (375-6). But her carriage arrives before she can find words; and Mr Knightley is not there to see "the tears running down her cheeks almost all the way home" while she takes no "trouble to check them, extraordinary as they were" (376).

Speaking of the moods in which several of Jane Austen's heroines, Emma among them, come to recognize their errors, C. S. Lewis remarks that 'the great abstract nouns of the classical English moralists are unblushingly and uncompromisingly used'.[5] Those nouns and their adjectives appear in force as Emma condemns herself for her behaviour at Box Hill: "mortification, deep concern,

---

3. Charles Lamb, 'On the Artificial Comedy of the Last Century' (1822) in *Essays of Elia*, Macmillan, London 1895, rev. edn 1945, p.201.
4. A. Walton Litz, *Jane Austen: A Study of Her Artistic Development*, p. 141.
5. C. S. Lewis, 'A Note on Jane Austen', *Essays in Criticism*, Vol. iv (1954), p. 363.

wretchedness, bare of rational satisfaction, [lack of] felicity, general conduct, severe reproach, conscience, scornful, ungracious, true contrition, penitence". There needs no cunning search for buried metaphors: these words are all used, in their natural senses, within three paragraphs (376-7). And Emma is not merely exploiting a vocabulary that suits her passing mood, as she had done in the earlier part of the Box Hill episode. When she thinks of it as a morning "more totally bare of *rational* satisfaction at the time, and more to be abhorred in recollection, than any she had ever passed" (377; my italics), the natural vigour of her expression is reinforced by her acceptance of that particular criterion. Again, when she acknowledges that she has been "ungracious" (377) to Miss Bates, she is relinquishing one of her favourite affectations. Both she and Mrs Elton have set much store by being "gracious" (22, 53, 260; 305, 321): but, from this point forward, the word is used only of Mrs Elton (453, 455).

After the original fiasco with Elton, the narrator laid a dry emphasis on Emma's wish to preserve appearances: thus, when she awoke next morning, she was much "more ready to see alleviations of the evil before her, and to depend on getting tolerably out of it" (138). After Box Hill, however, "time did not compose her" (376) and she "was just as determined when the morrow came" (377). She wonders whether "attention, in future, could do away the past" and looks forward—in exactly chosen words—to "a regular, equal, kindly intercourse" (377) with Miss Bates. When old Mrs Bates, in the only speech given her, assures Emma that Hetty will be there presently, "Emma seriously hoped she would. She had a moment's fear of Miss Bates keeping away from her" (378). After listening to Miss Bates' account of Jane Fairfax, Emma "spoke as she felt, with earnest regret and solicitude" (380). And, in taking leave, she repeats "every thing that she could venture to say of the good wishes which she really felt" (384).

Among the chief advantages of being a conventional heroine is that, if one truly repents, one is promptly and suitably rewarded. At first sight, Emma is rewarded in just this way. Jane Fairfax, certainly, is unresponsive to her overtures. But Miss Bates forgives her readily enough. And, when she arrives home, her father tells Mr Knightley of dear Emma's unfailing attentions to the Bateses:

Emma's colour was heightened by this unjust praise; and with a smile, and shake of the head, which spoke much, she looked at Mr. Knightley.— It seemed as if there were an instantaneous impression in her favour, as if his eyes received the truth from her's, and all that had passed of good in her feelings were at once caught and honoured.—He looked at her with a glow of regard. (385)

When Mr Knightley checks an impulse to kiss her hand, Emma thinks it from "some fancy or other" (386), not knowing that it is from the same union of jealousy and self-command as now takes him off to London. Their state, therefore, is not of such "perfect amity" (386) as she imagines. Yet he has forgiven her; and, in a fashion remote from Emma's theories, their conduct reveals an increasing if unacknowledged love. Meanwhile, as we have yet to learn, Harriet (who had been made unhappy at Box Hill because he gave so much of his attention to Jane Fairfax) is congratulating herself that he has just given her more of his time than he now gives Emma.

If there is an essential difference between the events of that morning and a more conventional pattern of repentance-and-reward, it does not lie in a few such passing ironies. It lies rather in Miss Bates' reception of Emma's journey to Canossa. For, though Emma is perfectly sincere, she is very full of her own sincerity. As she walks up the Bates' stairs, she moralizes on the difference between her present feelings and those of other visits. And, when Miss Bates does appear, "Emma's conscience told her that there was not the same cheerful volubility as before—less ease of look and manner" (378). We are not, I submit, to listen to Emma's conscience as attentively as Emma does. Although Miss Bates had been hurt, she now has as little care for the snub as for the apology. Her thoughts are all of Jane's illness and forthcoming departure, of the splendid prospects unfolded by good Mrs Elton, and of their grief in so sudden a parting. Of the Box Hill expedition, she says only that none of the others "'seemed very much to have enjoyed it. However, *I* shall always think it a very pleasant party, and feel extremely obliged to the kind friends who included me in it'" (381). We need not suspect Miss Bates of conscious irony: the comic implications of the episode are both higher and subtler. For all their importance to Emma and Mr Knightley, for all their interest to us, Emma's vagaries count for much less with those around her—and especially when those others are engaged in matters of serious concern.

II

Emma has little time to consider why Mr Knightley has gone away. For the next day brings news of the death of Mrs Churchill. "It was felt as such things must be felt", with "a degree of gravity and sorrow" (387); with a rueful acknowledgement that, after all, she had not been completely the hypochondriac; and, before very long, with an eye to its effects on Frank. Not for ten days, however, is its full effect on Frank discovered. In its portrayal of emotions in turmoil, the chapter where the secret engagement is made known ranks with any in the novel. As Weston escorts Emma to Randalls, one's sense of his anxiety is counterpointed with amusement at his idea of tact. As they return to Hartfield, he is back in his best Panglossian vein—but surely not without a sigh or two of relief. Mrs Weston's fears for Emma pass beyond mere anxiety and her relief shows no trace of self-concern. Since Emma has never really cared for Frank Churchill, " 'the simple truth' " (396) is less simple than Emma believes. Yet she does not care for him now: and, with this point established, Mrs Weston begins forgiving him the rest and exhorting Emma to do likewise.

When Weston first called for her at Hartfield, his whole manner suggestive of grave news, Emma's thoughts went at once to Brunswick Square, where she has one more dear friend than usual. Once these fears were set at rest, she found relief in a revival of her fancy: "Half a dozen natural children, perhaps—and poor Frank cut off" (393). Only when she reaches Mrs Weston is she told the news itself. In such a novel as this, her " 'Good God!' " (395) vouches for the intensity of her feelings. Their exact nature is declared a moment later: "Her mind was divided between two ideas—her own former conversations with him about Miss Fairfax; and poor Harriet" (395). Nothing Mrs Weston tells her can lessen her dismay on either count. All Highbury, she complains—though she is scarcely thinking of all Highbury—has been exposed to " 'a system of hypocrisy and deceit,—espionage, and treachery' " (399). Her one concession to Mrs Weston's pleas is that " 'if a woman can ever be excused for thinking only of herself, it is in a situation like Jane Fairfax's' " (400).

Emma's private reflections afterwards are essentially unaltered. She is still so angry with herself that, as she wryly admits, "it would have been dreadful" (403) if she could not also have been angry with Frank Churchill. She still maintains that "Jane Fairfax would have neither elevation nor happiness beyond her desert" (403). And, if she slightly accentuates the fact that Jane Fairfax needs no solicitude, that is because "poor Harriet was such an engrossing charge! There was little sympathy to be spared for any body else" (403). Hearing Harriet coming, she wishes that, like Mrs Weston's, her fears could prove unwarranted. But another very proper comparison escapes her. She does not think of the episode when she had nerved herself to tell Harriet that Mr Elton was to marry—only to find that Harriet could talk of nothing but meeting Robert Martin in a shop.

When Harriet enters cheerfully with the " 'very odd' " (404) news that Mr Weston has just passed on so confidentially, Emma feels extremely foolish. She has also to face such additional embarrassments from Harriet as an admiration for her ability to "'see into everybody's heart'" (404); a perfect astonishment that *anyone* could compare Frank Churchill to Mr Knightley; and an unwonted impudence: "'Oh! Miss Woodhouse, how you do forget!'" (406). Worst of all, perhaps, is Harriet's attempt to play the suave tactician. If Mr Knightley should not mind the disparity between herself and him, she must hope that dear Miss Woodhouse will not put difficulties in the way. And, taking a leaf from Uriah Heep's unwritten book, she adds, "'But you are too good for that, I am sure'" (407).

By this time, Emma has no room for embarrassment or anger. She has passed swiftly from a mysterious "terror" (405), through a growing "consternation" (407), to a thorough understanding of why she is dismayed: "It darted through her, with the speed of an arrow, that Mr. Knightley must marry no one but herself!" (408). Yet she finds "the resolution to sit and endure farther with calmness, with even apparent kindness" (408). Self-interest demands that Harriet's evidence be meticulously examined. Self-respect demands that she should conceal her own tremblings. But only through altruism could she remind herself, at such a time, that "Harriet had done nothing to forfeit the regard and interest which had been so voluntarily formed and maintained—or to deserve to be slighted by the person, whose counsels had never led her right" (408). And, when one accepts her "intentionally" as a necessary proviso, her conclusion reflects a noble generosity: "'Harriet, I will only venture to declare, that Mr. Knightley is the last man in the world, who would intentionally give any woman the idea of his feeling for her more than he really does'" (411).

In her reflections upon Darcy's letter, Elizabeth Bennet comes to a decisive turning-point: "'Till this moment, I never knew myself'" (*Pride and Prejudice*, p. 208); and she considers how her ignorance of herself has influenced her treatment of Darcy and Wickham. Both as a comment on her earlier behaviour and as the auspice of a happier future, Elizabeth's conclusion is borne out by the facts. And yet, while self-knowledge as here conceived may satisfy many critics, some novelists, and even the young Jane Austen, it is no more than a convenient fiction. In reality, one must insist, self-knowledge is not an absolute state to which a person attains in a single moment of insight. It is an erratic progress from one solution to a fresh problem, punctuated at best by moments of insight but too often marked by lapses and regressions, a stumbling progress ending only when life ends.

Like Elizabeth, Emma herself regards self-knowledge as a distinct, attainable goal. While she is discovering that Mr Knightley must marry no one but herself, her "own conduct, as well as her own heart, was before her in the same few minutes. She saw it all with a clearness which had never blessed her before" (408). After Harriet leaves her, she decides that her first endeavour must be "to understand, thoroughly understand her own heart"; and she soon reaches a new "knowledge of herself" (412). But, unlike Elizabeth, Emma is actually shown as coming only to a better, not a perfect, knowledge of herself and the meaning of her actions.

Emma is certainly right to conclude "that there never had been a time when she did not consider Mr. Knightley as infinitely the superior, or when his regard for her had not been infinitely the most dear . . . and, in short, that she had never really cared for Frank Churchill at all!" (412). She is right to think that, having always known that she was "*first* with Mr. Knightley, first in interest and affection" (415), she had taken his regard as her due and enjoyed it without reflection. And she is right, above all, in her estimate of her own motives: "With insufferable vanity had she believed herself in the secret of everybody's feelings; with unpardonable arrogance proposed to arrange everybody's destiny" (412-13). The misunderstandings that survive in spite of these important discoveries are less concerned with her self, as narrowly conceived, than with certain relationships between that self and the world about her.

She continues, in the first place, to over-estimate her past influence on others, most notably in her belief that she might have put an early end to Harriet's current attachment. On the face of it, Emma's opinion is supported by Harriet's insistent claims (404-11) that, without Emma's encouragement, she would never have dared think of Mr Knightley. But consider the speech (342) to which Harriet chiefly refers. No doubt Emma had meant to be encouraging; but, taking warning from their previous misadventure with Mr Elton, she actually spoke far more cautiously than she or Harriet remembers. *She* has forgotten the doubts and reservations she then expressed because she is in a mood of violent self-recrimination. Harriet has forgotten them because it has never suited her to remember. Since that time, Harriet has repeatedly found encouragement where none was intended. And, even now, while Harriet is trying to justify her hopes, there is a certain brittleness in everything she says. She is glib enough when she refers to Emma's past encouragement and tries to ensure her future acquiescence; but, when she speaks of Mr Knightley, she is almost inarticulate, searching assiduously and in vain for words that will give substance to a figment:

"But I hope, Miss Woodhouse, that supposing—that if—strange as it may appear—. But you know they were your own words, that *more* wonderful things had happened, matches of *greater* disparity had taken place than between Mr. Frank Churchill and me; and, therefore, it seems as if such a thing even as this, may have occurred before—and if I should be so fortunate, beyond expression, as to—if Mr. Knightley should really—if *he* does not mind the disparity, I hope, dear Miss Woodhouse, you will not set yourself against it, and try to put difficulties in the way." (407)

Not even Miss Woodhouse could have prevented the indulgence of such airy sentiments, such glittering aspirations, as Harriet vests in Mr Knightley; and yet Harriet remains dimly aware that such hopes are not for her fulfilling.

After Harriet leaves her, Emma pursues these questions in another direction. She is much afraid that the marriage may take place; that, by accidentally causing Harriet to think of Mr Knightley, she has induced her to act in a manner that may have attracted him; and that "he would never have known Harriet at all but for her folly" (413). Although the last point might be debated, the other two are quite untenable, resting on a thoroughly misguided idea of Mr Knightley. Emma cannot know, of course, that most of the gestures in which Harriet has found encouragement —his seeking her company, praising her simplicity, and privately acknowledging his reluctance to go to London—are really expressions of his belief that *she* is lost to him. She should know, however, that Mr Knightley is no such fool as to marry Harriet Smith.

The same misjudgement of Mr Knightley, the sense that even he has proved incalculable, is a mainspring of the large speculations into which Emma is now driven: "Was it new [she wonders] for any thing in this world to be unequal, inconsistent, incongruous— or for chance and circumstance (as second causes) to direct the human fate?" (413). These feelings declare themselves in more concrete terms when, influenced not merely by Mrs Weston's touching account of Jane Fairfax's trials of conscience but also by her own fears for Mr Knightley, she renounces her belief that Jane Fairfax had been guided, in the least degree, by calculations of self-interest: "'Poor girl!' said Emma again. 'She loves him then excessively, I suppose. It must have been from attachment only, that she could be led to form the engagement. Her affection must have overpowered her judgment'" (419). In her consternation, Emma overstates these discoveries. The outburst about Jane Fairfax meets a mild answer from Mrs Weston: "'Yes, I have no doubt of her being extremely attached to him'" (419). And Emma's larger fears are answered, indirectly, by Jane Fairfax's stern but not unhopeful belief that "'it can be only weak, irresolute characters, (whose happiness must be always at the mercy of chance,) ...'" (373).

The very humility that goes with Emma's sudden access of "self-knowledge" leads her into further errors. She admits how little she has deserved Mr Knightley's long-standing concern for her and how often she has been "negligent or perverse, slighting his advice, or even wilfully opposing him, insensible of half his merits, and quarrelling with him because he would not acknowledge her false and insolent estimate of her own" (415). Though Emma has needed to be humbled, Mr Knightley does not warrant such idolatry as this. By the same token, Emma's new humility induces a yearning for the past when Mr Knightley had acted as a second and more effective father. No doubt this relationship had often been delightful. Yet Emma should not continue to think like Peter Pan—or Isabella Knightley.

Before another day has passed, she will have been relieved of the need to acknowledge chance as absolute, to renounce her own rights as an individual, and to yearn for a perpetuated childhood. But she is not saved merely by a timely proposal of marriage. By the end of this same evening, Emma is already finding her own way to more tenable conclusions. As later events will show, her self-knowledge still falls short of that state which I have called a convenient fiction. Yet, without Jane Fairfax's experience of suffering, she approaches her resoluteness:

> ... the only source whence any thing like consolation or composure could be drawn, was in the resolution of her own better conduct, and the hope that, however inferior in spirit and gaiety might be the following and every future winter of her life to the past, it would yet find her more rational, more acquainted with herself, and leave her less to regret when it were gone. (423)

The narrator steps between Emma and the reader just after Mr Knightley has proposed: "What did she say?—Just what she ought, of course. A lady always does" (431). This intervention has very often been associated with other occasions on which Jane Austen resorts to 'telling' where critical fashion would recommend a 'showing'; and it has been suggested that she is evading speeches or incidents that surpass her powers. But Professor Armour Craig insists that 'Jane Austen is not unequal to providing the whispered rhetoric of so tender a scene. The drama is simply elsewhere for her.'[6] He goes on to argue that Jane Austen's 'drama' lies—no less at such a moment—in the endless, subtle relations (and discrepancies) between actual conduct and imputed feelings.

6. G. Armour Craig, 'Jane Austen's *Emma*: The Truths and Disguises of Human Disclosure' in R. A. Brower and Richard Poirier (eds), *In Defense of Reading*, p. 237.

The whole episode in which Mr Knightley stumbles his way unexpectedly into making a proposal and Emma is at first too astonished to accept might be examined, phrase by phrase, as an epitome of these things. But we have previously looked at the implications of the simple phrase, "as a friend" (429). And we have seen enough of the motives that lead each of them into misconstructions: that lead Emma, on seeing him out of spirits, to suppose "that he had perhaps been communicating his plans to his brother, and was pained by the manner in which they had been received" (424); that lead her, on discovering that he has somehow learned of Frank Churchill's engagement, to suppose that "he might have called at Mrs. Goddard's in his way" (425); that lead Mr Knightley, on hearing Emma talk sorrowfully of having "'been doomed to blindness'" (425), to suppose that she has actually been jilted; and that lead him, on hearing that she has never loved Frank Churchill, to set about an instantaneous reappraisal of that "'favourite of fortune'" (428). Though the whole episode is instinct with both poignancy and amusement, one would not wish laboriously to record each heart-beat or to underline each sally of Jane Austen's wit.

One must emphasize, however, how magnanimously they both behave. In spite of Emma's past scorn for his solicitude and with nothing whatever to revive his buried hopes, Mr Knightley has returned from London as soon as she seemed to be in need. And, convinced by now that he has succumbed to Harriet and is struggling to confess it, Emma in turn rises nobly to the demands of an intolerable occasion:

Emma could not bear to give him pain. He was wishing to confide in her—perhaps to consult her;—cost her what it would, she would listen. She might assist his resolution, or reconcile him to it; she might give just praise to Harriet, or, by representing to him his own independence, relieve him from that state of indecision, which must be more intolerable than any alternative to such a mind as his.—They had reached the house.

"You are going in, I suppose," said he.

"No"—replied Emma—quite confirmed by the depressed manner in which he still spoke—"I should like to take another turn. Mr. Perry is not gone." And, after proceeding a few steps, she added—"I stopped you ungraciously, just now . . ." (429)

A few moments later, the same magnanimity unites with Emma's fundamental good sense when she pauses before answering his proposal. With a rueful glance at her former absurd fancies about love, she sees how thoroughly she lacks that "heroism of sentiment" which might lead her, at such a moment, to plead Harriet's cause or even "to refuse him at once and for ever, without vouchsafing any motive, because he could not marry them both". She thinks of Harriet "with pain and with contrition" but can do nothing for her beyond enabling her to take refuge in Brunswick Square. Yet she has every right "to rejoice that Harriet's secret had not escaped her, and to resolve that it need not and should not" (431). Although Emma would choose to begin her new life on a footing of simple frankness, Harriet has a higher claim. Harriet's second unfortunate attachment, unlike her first, will never become "an offering to conjugal unreserve" (282).

Although their progress towards mutual understanding is not complete, both Emma and Mr Knightley are shown as having conquered their worst prejudices, as growing increasingly worthy of each other, and as learning to treat each other with true affection. That affection differs sharply from the condescending benevolence of Mr Knightley's former attitude: "'Emma knows I never flatter her'" (11); "'I should like to see Emma in love, and in some doubt of a return'" (41). It differs, again, from the mere subservience of "'always first and always right'" (84) which Emma had thought to be a lover's part. The narrator may well comment, then, that "this one half hour had given to each the same precious certainty of being beloved, had cleared from each the same degree of ignorance, jealousy, or distrust" (432).

III

"She was his own Emma, by hand and word" (433). Since *Emma* is not a fairytale, Jane Austen does not end there but spends fifty pages securing their affection before avowing their future happiness. Those pages are marked by the resolution of outstanding issues, chiefly affecting Harriet and Mr Woodhouse; by reappraisals of questions formerly in dispute; and by an undercurrent of small endearments and good-hearted ridicule.

Only a little while before, when her future seemed to lie in ruins, Emma had wished only for the perpetuation of the old life at Hartfield, with Mr Knightley freed of Harriet and continuing as their visitor and friend. This passing impulse of nostalgia has too often been confused with the very different state of mind in which Emma decides that not even marriage can justify her deserting her father. Those who regard Emma's unwillingness to leave her father as one and unchanging, as the reflection of emotional immaturity and worse,[7] are influenced, perhaps, by our twentieth-century dislike for 'living with the in-laws'. They are forgetting that, whatever its

7. *See* for example Edmund Wilson, 'A Long Talk about Jane Austen' in Ian Watt (ed.), *Jane Austen*, pp. 38-9.

merits, our attitude is almost without historical precedent and was certainly not accepted in Jane Austen's England. And, in terms of this novel, they are aligning themselves with Mrs Elton: "'Shocking plan, living together. It would never do. She knew a family near Maple Grove who had tried it, and been obliged to separate before the end of the first quarter'" (469).

"'Nobody, who has not been in the interior of a family, can say what the difficulties of any individual of that family may be'" (146). The spinster daughter of Mrs Cassandra Austen[8] needs no reminder of what it is to live always with one's parents, let alone one's parents-in-law. Accordingly, when Mr Knightley tells Emma that —since "a transplantation would be a risk of her father's comfort, perhaps even of his life" (448-9)—he is willing to live with them, Emma is:

... sensible of all the affection it evinced. She felt that, in quitting Donwell, he must be sacrificing a great deal of independence of hours and habits; that in living constantly with her father, and in no house of his own, there would be much, very much, to be borne with. (449)

Mr Knightley's insistence that he has already been "thinking it over most deeply, most intently" (448) indicates that he, too, knows what is entailed. In accepting the disadvantages of their least unsatisfactory course, they are behaving as rational beings.

Obviously the scheme cannot be put to Mr Woodhouse while he is anxious about Mrs Weston, whose pregnancy is far advanced. And, though Harriet troubles Emma's conscience, that problem, too, must lie in abeyance until the girl returns from London. Thus Emma is granted "a holiday of spirits" (452), and Jane Austen gives herself an opportunity to take up other issues.

In respect of the information it discloses and the light it sheds on its writer, Frank Churchill's long explanatory letter has already served us well. It is valuable also for the comments it evokes from Emma and Mr Knightley. Her response is as amusing as it is predictable. She begins by regretting that, at such a time as this, it "must be waded through" (436). But the sight of her own name quickens her interest and, by the time she finishes reading it, she is full of the sentimental forgiveness expressed in her "so" and "so" and "so":

... though it was impossible not to feel that he had been wrong, yet he had been less wrong than she had supposed—and he had suffered, and was very

8. Mr Geoffrey Gorer has assembled many scattered references to Jane Austen's mother. The picture resulting is of a domineering hypochondriac. *See* his 'Poor Honey—Some Notes on Jane Austen and Her Mother' in *The Danger of Equality*, pp. 248-64.

sorry—and he was so grateful to Mrs. Weston, and so much in love with Miss Fairfax, and she was so happy herself, that there was no being severe; ... (444)

Mr Knightley has less difficulty in tempering his rapture. When he agrees to read the letter, it is for a characteristic reason, characteristically expressed: "'as it seems a matter of justice, it shall be done'" (444). Yet his next comment, on Frank Churchill's "'fine complimentary opening'", exactly captures his own altered state of mind: "'But it is his way. One man's style must not be the rule of another's. We will not be severe'" (445). On the one hand, it is much for Mr Knightley to forsake his old prescriptiveness about what "a man" should do and to adopt this permissive distinction between one man and another. On the other hand, his use of "will" —like that of "shall" in the preceding comment—testifies to the effort his concession requires.[9]

Mr Knightley's surviving austerities are most important in his *rapprochement* with Emma. He tempers them whenever he honestly can, and Emma comes to meet him. They each admit to having been prejudiced when they originally quarrelled about Frank Churchill. They are able to agree that he is "'the child of good fortune'" (448). And their final comments show that they can now approach agreement without feeling obliged to sink—much less to flaunt—their inevitable differences of age and temperament:

> "You do not appear so well satisfied with his letter as I am; but still you must, at least I hope you must, think the better of him for it. I hope it does him some service with you."
> "Yes, certainly it does. He has had great faults, faults of inconsideration and thoughtlessness; and I am very much of his opinion in thinking him likely to be happier than he deserves: but still as he is, beyond a doubt, really attached to Miss Fairfax, and will soon, it may be hoped, have the advantage of being constantly with her, I am very ready to believe his character will improve, and acquire from her's the steadiness and delicacy of principle that it wants." (448)

Frank Churchill's last appearance in person bears out these opinions. His lingering on Jane Fairfax's beauty and his pleasure in Emma's friendship with her testify to his warm affections. But, in his willingness to revive the joke about Perry's carriage (despite Jane's evident embarrassment), he is as thoughtless as ever. It is here that Emma judges herself unfairly. Had she been in his position, she would undoubtedly, as she now says, have seen its amusing side. But, however often she has been blind to other people's

9. Dr Chapman remarks, in another connection, that 'J. A.'s use of *shall* and *will* is strict' (*Letters*, note on No. 143).

motives, she has never shared his fondness for persisting in the face of known resentment. Even at Box Hill, when her conduct most resembled his, she came quickly to such a trial by conscience as Frank Churchill could never so much as imagine.

Emma's "sense of past injustice towards Miss Fairfax" (421) has aroused some of her bitterest regrets; she has acknowledged that she should certainly have "endeavoured to find a friend there instead of in Harriet Smith" (421); and she has long since begun to think of her as "Jane" (363 ff.). Jane Fairfax, on her side, has sent friendly and apologetic messages through Mrs Weston. And, feeling "the resemblance of their present situations increasing every other motive of good will" (452), Emma goes to visit her.

Throughout this episode, Jane Austen relies on Mrs Elton to conceal the fact that—because neither Emma nor Jane can speak openly of "their present situations"—there is little for them to discuss. That lady makes it her business graciously to transmit Mrs Smallridge's messages of forgiveness; anxiously to parade her knowledge of the engagement, on the assumption that Miss Woodhouse has not been told; and eagerly to recall that not everyone had been allowed visit Jane Fairfax's sick-bed. And, torn between self-importance and irrational resentment, she even declaims on the cares of clerical life. An impressive performance, even by her standards, it is crowned by her malicious allusions to Box Hill: for she supposes that Emma, having been seriously attached to Frank Churchill, must by now be distressed by his long absence from Hartfield; and she gleefully rubs salt into this imaginary wound. Emma, all this while, is quietly conforming to other standards. She does not even hint that she knows more than Mrs Elton imagines. And, in the face of overwhelming temptations, "Emma would not have smiled for the world" (456).

For the greater part of the visit, then, Emma and Jane are able only to exchange friendly glances and quietly resist Mrs Elton's attempts to re-open old wounds. But, both at meeting and at parting, their growing liking for each other declares itself plainly. Jane now shows the "consciousness, animation, and warmth" that she has been obliged to conceal, and speaks in a "very feeling tone" of her pleasure in Emma's gesture. And Emma, silenced by Mrs Elton, tries "to compress all her friendly and all her congratulatory sensations into a very, very earnest shake of the hand" (453).

Emma's change of heart can also be discerned in the far-reaching implications of a phrase which—like "amiable" or "fancy"—epitomizes a whole aspect of the novel. Jane speaks, we are told, "with a blush and an hesitation which Emma thought infinitely more becoming to her than all the elegance of all her usual composure" (459). So prompted, one recalls how Emma used to insist on Miss Fairfax's "elegance" (e.g., 171, 194, 199). Indeed when Jane Fairfax had arrived in Highbury, Emma had not only been so "particularly struck" (167) by her elegance that she mentions it six times in this one page but had also made her own principle explicit: "It was a style of beauty, of which elegance was the reigning character, and as such, she must, in honour, by all her principles, admire it:—elegance, which, whether of person or of mind, she saw so little in Highbury" (167).

There has, in fact, been so little elegance in Highbury that Emma has given this favourite principle some unexpected applications. For a short time, she is persuaded that Harriet, of all people, "wanted only a little more knowledge and elegance to be quite perfect" (23). (By the time she paints Harriet's portrait, she feels that she must add not only "a little more height" but also "considerably more elegance": 47.) She is even less discriminating when she suggests merely that "true elegance was sometimes wanting" (135) in Mr Elton and that he is much her own "inferior in talent, and all the elegancies of mind" (136).

With the arrival of Jane Fairfax, however, elegance acquires a stricter meaning. When Frank Churchill seems to imply that, by the standards of the fashionable world, even Miss Fairfax is not especially gifted with "elegance" (194), Emma is dismayed by a sense of her own rusticity. But she soon decides that he is no proper arbiter: "his indifference to a confusion of rank, bordered too much on inelegance of mind" (198). In this mood of confidence, Emma's concern for elegance reaches its apogee. The mere word can be used as occasion requires. After meeting Mrs Elton, Emma determines to describe her only in "the nothing-meaning terms of being 'elegantly dressed, and very pleasing'" (270); and she abides by that determination (271, 281). But true elegance is beyond most of her acquaintance: apart from Jane Fairfax—and doubtless herself—Mrs Weston, whose manners are marked by "'propriety, simplicity, and elegance'" (278), alone can qualify. As for Mrs Elton, Emma "suspected that there was no elegance;—ease, but not elegance" (270). And, on this point at least, Emma is fully supported by one of the narrator's most cutting phrases: Mrs Elton arrives at the Hartfield dinner-party "as elegant as lace and pearls could make her" (292).

The narrator may agree with Emma, but Highbury takes a different view. Even before her arrival, Miss Hawkins "was, by some means or other, discovered to have every recommendation of person and mind; to be handsome, elegant, highly accomplished, and perfectly amiable" (181). Closer acquaintance makes little difference: "dear Mrs. Elton, how elegant she looks!—Beautiful lace!—Now we all follow in her train. Quite the queen of the evening!'" (329). Meanwhile the lady herself sets up as Highbury's arbiter on all points of elegance. Even though dear Jane is, so unfortunately, not versed in the harp, her patroness will ensure that she is saved from any family "'not moving in a certain circle, or able to command the elegancies of life'" (301). The Smallridge establishment, of course, is eminently suitable. In a passage quite pervaded by cheap Eltonian jargon, poor Miss Bates trots out that "'liberal and elegant'" establishment, those "'elegant sweet children'" (382), for Emma's approval and her own solace.

What is Emma to do? She can scarcely cast aspersions on a stranger merely because she shows a suspicious haste to grab her governess and is Mrs Elton's bosom-friend. Nor can she hope, more generally, to convince her neighbours that "elegance", as Mrs Elton conceives it, is a shoddy disguise for self-seeking vulgarity. She knows by now that Highbury requires none of her guidance and that its compliments, which she had been taught to accept as her peculiar right, are so idly bestowed as to be worthless. As far as Highbury is concerned, she quietly abides by these discoveries. For her own part, meanwhile, she has learnt to value qualities less external than those to which "elegance"—like "amiability" and "agreeableness" —ordinarily pays tribute. Emma's eventual answer, therefore, is to concede Mrs Elton all the elegance she cares to claim. As early as the ball, Emma had wondered "what Frank's first opinion of Mrs. Elton might be; how he was affected by the studied elegance of her dress, and her smiles of graciousness" (320-1). By the close of the novel, she is promising Mr Knightley not to emulate "'the elegant terseness of Mrs. Elton, by calling you Mr. K.'" (463). And she rightly concludes that Jane Fairfax's blush and hesitation are "infinitely more becoming to her than all the elegance of all her usual composure" (459).

Yet we are not asked to accept that the old, outrageous Emma has expired in the odour of perfect sanctity. When she visits Jane Fairfax, Emma is thinking with satisfaction of "the resemblance of their present situations" but is obliged, on her father's account, to let it remain "a *secret* satisfaction" (452). In such a position, a lesser woman might weakly confide in Jane Fairfax or, no less weakly, leave the whole subject of engagements alone. Not Emma! She not only encourages Jane Fairfax to confide in *her* but cheerfully compliments her on her frankness: "'Thank you, thank you.—This is just what I wanted to be assured of.—Oh! if you knew how much I love every thing that is decided and open'" (460).

The birth of Anna Weston gives rise to another searching

conversation between Emma and Mr Knightley. Emma's particular satisfaction that the child is a girl is not simply a reminder of her old love of match-making. The suggestion that she "would not acknowledge" (461) any such intentions implies, I think, that she is smiling ruefully at her own former proclivities and that Jane Austen's real irony is delayed a moment longer. For, thinking of Anna as Mrs Weston's *next* pupil, Emma unblushingly decides that "it would be quite a pity that any one who so well knew how to teach, should not have their powers in exercise again" (461).

When Emma gives Mr Knightley the benefit of this opinion, supporting it with a solemn analogy from Madame de Genlis, his reply shows how he has learnt to cope with his Emma. He tells the truth as plainly as ever but exaggerates it enough to make Emma laugh at herself instead of taking offence at him:

". . . she will indulge her even more than she did you, and believe that she does not indulge her at all. It will be the only difference."

"Poor child!" cried Emma; "at that rate, what will become of her?"

"Nothing very bad.—The fate of thousands. She will be disagreeable in infancy, and correct herself as she grows older. I am losing all my bitterness against spoilt children, my dearest Emma. I, who am owing all my happiness to *you*, would not it be horrible ingratitude in me to be severe on them?"

Emma laughed, and replied. . . (461-2)

As the conversation continues, it grows more serious, as indeed it must. At the time of his proposal, Mr Knightley had confessed that, "'I have blamed you, and lectured you, and you have borne it as no other woman in England would have borne it'" (430). But this point was then lost among more pressing considerations. When Mr Knightley returns to it, Emma responds generously to his generosity:

"My interference was quite as likely to do harm as good. It was very natural for you to say, what right has he to lecture me?—and I am afraid very natural for you to feel that it was done in a disagreeable manner. I do not believe I did you any good. The good was all to myself, by making you an object of the tenderest affection to me. . . ."

"I am sure you were of use to me," cried Emma. "I was very often influenced rightly by you—oftener than I would own at the time. I am very sure you did me good. And if poor little Anna Weston is to be spoiled, it will be the greatest humanity in you to do as much for her as you have done for me, except falling in love with her when she is thirteen." (462)

If this conversation exhibits Mr Knightley's new understanding of spoilt children (cf. 37, 99), the next exhibits Emma's new understanding of plain speaking. For, as is implied by Mr Knightley's intercessions, his brother is "'rather cool'" (464) in Emma's praise.

But Mr Knightley's efforts are not needed. Emma now r ecognizes that sincerity, even so outspoken and untimely a sincerity as this, is more serviceable than all the amiable flourishes of a Frank Churchill, much less a Philip Elton: when she declares, "'He writes like a sensible man. . . . I honour his sincerity'" (464), she is announcing one of the chief discoveries of her twenty-second year. So, too, when she accepts John Knightley's wish that she may eventually become worthy of his brother. With these remarks, moreover, she brings *us* back to our original point of departure. In the Introduction to this study I suggested that this passage is a paradigm of the novel as it has usually been read; but that, while Emma does well to regard herself so humbly, the novel does not really accede to her assessment of her relationship with Mr Knightley; and that, while Emma needed to learn more respect for "sensible men", we need not regard "sensible" as Jane Austen's epithet for absolute virtue.

In these closing episodes, Jane Austen still writes with the "sort of serious smile" (464) that she attributes to Emma. Even a passing sally can cut deep into the novel, as when Emma urges Mr Knightley to ask William Larkins' consent before removing to Hartfield or as when she foresees her father's reception of their news: "'I wish I may not sink into "poor Emma" with him at once'" (464). For a profounder humour, however, one turns to longer passages: to the whole discussion of spoilt children (461-3); to the whole discussion of Harriet's engagement (470-5); and, ultimately, to the novel as a whole, a novel whose riches seem inexhaustible.

Harriet's engagement to Robert Martin is a remarkable instance of the ramifications of Jane Austen's comic art. On the face of it, Emma is too easily released from the consequences of her folly and arrogance. And yet, as I have previously suggested, her influence on Harriet is less than she supposes. Despite Harriet's claim that she now knows better than "'to care for Mr. Martin'" (411), every reference to that young man has found her keenly interested. And Harriet's engagement is no happy accident. Mr Knightley has long been studying her attitude to young Martin. Unwilling to work against Emma behind her back, he has spoken to Harriet only in terms so general that she thinks he is pleading his own cause. But, when Emma arranges for Harriet to stay with Isabella, he pockets his scruples enough to have Robert Martin "'take charge of some papers which I was wanting to send to John'" (471). The rest follows very easily.

When Mr Knightley tells Emma of Harriet's engagement, he sincerely admits her right to be less pleased than he, while hoping that their opinions will one day coincide. But Emma confesses that she had acted like a fool. The rest of their conversation is punctuated by affectionate sallies. Disclaiming all detailed knowledge, he avers that men have no interest in "'minute particulars'" and "'deal only in the great'" (472). And Emma, anxious as never before to allow no conceivable ambiguity, pretends he is bemused: "'It was not Harriet's hand that he was certain of—it was the dimensions of some famous ox'" (473). Jane Austen, even now, has only just begun. Mr Knightley praises Harriet for just such virtues, gentility excepted, as Emma had originally claimed for her; and, when the legend of Harriet's gentility is exploded, Mr Knightley will feel no sense of triumph. For his catalogue of Harriet's virtues ends in the declaration:

"—Much of this, I have no doubt, she may thank you for."
  "Me!" cried Emma, shaking her head.—"Ah! poor Harriet!"
  She checked herself, however, and submitted quietly to a little more praise than she deserved. (474-5)

Emma submits quietly because, while feeling "the pain of being obliged to practise concealment towards him" (463), she still owes it to Harriet not to tell him the whole story. The easy conclusion is that, through ignorance of the circumstances, Mr Knightley causes Emma to feel a richly deserved embarrassment.

But why only "a *little* more praise than she deserved"? By an avenue entirely unexpected, Emma actually has done Harriet good. She had advised Harriet to "'be observant'" of the man they had agreed not to name, to "'let his behaviour be the guide of your sensations'" (342). Although Harriet over-simplifies this advice, she claims to have acted by it: "'You told me to observe him carefully, and let his behaviour be the rule of mine—and so I have'" (411). One cannot begin to envisage a Harriet-cum-Knightley! Yet, in managing not to blurt out her idol's name and in behaving so as to earn his hearty commendation, Harriet shows distinctly better sense than she originally brought with her to Hartfield.

Mr Knightley cannot know that he was Harriet's model; and Emma is still so concerned about having misled Harriet, so happy in the outcome of Harriet's misadventures, that she is "fit for nothing rational" (475). Beyond the fact itself, "it must ever be unintelligible to Emma" (481). Here, as much as anywhere in the novel, Jane Austen's "serious smile" can be discerned. It is fitting that, at the last, Harriet's behaviour should escape Mr Knightley's understanding and defy Emma's calculations. Both Emma and Mr Knightley know themselves better than they did. But, if perfect self-knowledge recedes like a mirage, the knowledge of others' motives is still harder to attain. Even a Harriet, Jane Austen seems to be saying, is ultimately inviolable.

Even a Harriet: and even a Mr Woodhouse. When Emma accepts Mr Knightley's scheme of living at Hartfield, they believe that her father's resistance will not prove insuperable. While Mr Knightley sings Emma's praises to him, she and Mrs Weston begin putting the whole plan "in the most serviceable light—first, as a settled, and secondly, as a good one—well aware of the nearly equal importance of the two recommendations to Mr. Woodhouse's mind" (467). As he grudgingly admits, the marriage, under the agreed arrangement, offers *him* nothing but advantage. In his last struggles to have the wedding itself indefinitely postponed, he has no motives more real than neurotic fancies and a selfish fear of change. To understand such fancies, however, is by no means to dispel them; and those who had thought him manageable make no further progress. When Emma and Mr Knightley are "befriended" by events, it is "not by any sudden illumination of Mr. Woodhouse's mind, or any wonderful change of his nervous system, but by the operation of the same system in another way" (483). The decisive occurrence is as trivial as his response is absurd. Those who break into poultry-yards may break into houses. Donwell may care for itself but Hartfield needs protection. And what more sturdy watch-dog than brave Mr Knightley?

"The wedding was very much like other weddings, where the parties have no taste for finery or parade" (484). Mrs Elton's contempt for their proceedings is exceeded only by her pessimism about their future. But the last guarantee of their happiness lies in the very restraint of Jane Austen's last phrase. In all the novels of her maturity, "felicity" is among the qualities most valued. It is not the rapture of a seventeenth-century mystic but an earthly serenity, not a vision of 'orient and immortal wheat' but a prospect of Donwell Abbey. As *Emma* nears its close, each of the principals sees "felicity" as lying in the love, companionship, and mutual trust of marriage (428, 475); and Mrs Weston foretells "a union of the highest promise of felicity" (468). It is right that they should feel so. Yet the narrator speaks of "happiness" and says nothing of "felicity". Even in such a moment, Jane Austen's voice is raised only a little above its natural pitch:

. . . the wishes, the hopes, the confidence, the predictions of the small band of true friends who witnessed the ceremony, were fully answered in the perfect happiness of the union.

SELECT BIBLIOGRAPHY

A: EDITIONS

Frequent reference is made to the following:
The novels, in The Oxford Illustrated Jane Austen, edited by R. W. Chapman:

Sense and Sensibility [1923], 3rd edn. London 1933; reprinted 1960.

Pride and Prejudice [1923], 3rd edn. London 1932; reprinted 1959.

Mansfield Park [1923], 3rd edn. London 1934; reprinted 1960.

Emma [1923], 3rd edn. London 1933; reprinted 1960.

Northanger Abbey and *Persuasion* [1923], 3rd edn. London 1933; reprinted 1959.

Minor Works [1954], reprinted with revisions. London 1963.

Chapman, R. W. (ed.), *Jane Austen's Letters to her sister Cassandra and others* [1932], 2nd edn. London 1952; reprinted with corrections, 1959.

B: BIBLIOGRAPHIES AND CHECKLISTS

Chapman, R. W., *Jane Austen: A Critical Bibliography.* Oxford 1953; 2nd edn, 1955.

Keynes, G. L., *Jane Austen: A Bibliography.* London 1929.

Link, F. M., *The Reputation of Jane Austen in the Twentieth Century, with an Annotated Enumerative Bibliography of Austen Criticism from 1811 to June, 1957.* Unpublished dissertation, Boston University, 1958. Available on microfilm. A checklist of criticism published after June 1957 will be found in the pages of the *Philological Quarterly.*

C: BIOGRAPHIES

Austen-Leigh, James Edward, *A Memoir of Jane Austen* [1871]. Ed. R. W. Chapman, London 1926.

Austen-Leigh, W. and R. A., *Jane Austen: Her Life and Letters.* London 1913.

Jenkins, Elizabeth, *Jane Austen: A Biography.* London 1938.

Lascelles, Mary, *Jane Austen and Her Art.* London 1939.

D: Criticism

The following is a selective list of some of the more useful studies, including all those to which I have made formal reference. Further references will be found in Link (*see* B *above*).

Babb, Howard S., *Jane Austen's Novels: The Fabric of Dialogue*. Columbus, Ohio 1962.

Booth, Wayne C., *The Rhetoric of Fiction*. Chicago 1961.

Bradbrook, Frank W., 'Dr. Johnson and Jane Austen'. *Notes and Queries*, Vol. ccv (1960), pp. 108-12.

——, *Jane Austen: 'Emma'*. London 1961.

——, *Jane Austen and Her Predecessors*. Cambridge 1966.

Bradley, A. C., 'Jane Austen: A Lecture'. *Essays and Studies*, Vol. ii (1911), pp. 7-36.

Brontë, Charlotte in C. K. Shorter, *The Brontës: Life and Letters*. 2 vols, London 1908. For letters to G. H. Lewes (12 and 18 January 1848), Vol. i, pp. 387-8; and to W. H. Williams (12 April 1850), Vol. ii, pp. 127-8.

Brower, Reuben Arthur, 'Light and Bright and Sparkling: Irony and Fiction in *Pride and Prejudice*' in his *The Fields of Light: An Experiment in Critical Reading*. London 1951, pp. 164-81.

Bullitt, John and Bate W. J., 'Distinctions between Fancy and Imagination in Eighteenth-Century English Criticism'. *Modern Language Notes*, Vol. lx (1945), pp. 8-15.

Cecil, David, 'Jane Austen: The Leslie Stephen Lecture'. Cambridge 1935.

Chapman, R. W., *Jane Austen: Facts and Problems*. Oxford 1948.

Child, Harold, 'Jane Austen'. *Cambridge History of English Literature*, Vol. xii (1915), pp. 231-44.

Craig, G. Armour, 'Jane Austen's *Emma*: The Truths and Disguises of Human Disclosure' in R. A. Brower and W. R. Poirier (eds), *In Defense of Reading: A Reader's Approach to Literary Criticism*. New York 1962, pp. 235-55.

Craik, W. A., *Jane Austen: The Six Novels*. London 1965.

Farrer, Reginald, 'Jane Austen, *ob.* July 18, 1817'. *Quarterly Review*, Vol. ccxxviii (1917), pp. 1-30.

Gorer, Geoffrey, 'Poor Honey—Some Notes on Jane Austen and Her Mother' in his *The Danger of Equality*. London 1966, pp. 248-64.

Harding, D. W., 'Regulated Hatred: An Aspect of the Work of Jane Austen'. *Scrutiny*, Vol. viii (1940), pp. 346-62.

Harvey, W. J., 'The Plot of *Emma*'. *Essays in Criticism*, Vol. xvii (1967), pp. 48-63.

Hughes, R. E., 'The Education of Emma Woodhouse'. *Nineteenth-Century Fiction*, Vol. xvi (1961), pp. 69-74.

Kettle, Arnold, '*Emma*' in Ian Watt (ed.), *Jane Austen*, q.v., pp. 112-23.

Lamb, Charles, 'On the Artificial Comedy of the Last Century' (1822) in his *Essays of Elia*. London 1895. 1945 edn, pp. 197-206.

Lascelles, Mary, *Jane Austen and Her Art*. London 1939.

Lewis, C. S., 'A Note on Jane Austen'. *Essays in Criticism*, Vol. iv (1954), pp. 359-71.

Liddell, Robert, *The Novels of Jane Austen*. London 1963.

Litz, A. Walton, *Jane Austen: A Study of Her Artistic Development*. London 1965.

Mudrick, Marvin, *Jane Austen: Irony as Defense and Discovery*. Princeton 1952.

Page, Norman, 'Standards of Excellence: Jane Austen's Language'. *Review of English Literature*, Vol. vii (1966), pp. 91-8.

Poirier, Richard, 'Transatlantic Configurations: Mark Twain and Jane Austen' in his *A World Elsewhere: The Place of Style in American Literature*. London 1967, pp. 144-207.

Schorer, Mark, 'The Humiliation of Emma Woodhouse' in Ian Watt (ed.), *Jane Austen*, q.v., pp. 98-111.

[Scott, Walter], '*Emma*'. *Quarterly Review*, Vol. xiv (1815), pp. 188-201.

Shannon, Edgar F., '*Emma*: Character and Construction'. *PMLA*, Vol. lxxi (1956), pp. 637-50.

Shepperson, Archibald B., *The Novel in Motley: A History of the Burlesque Novel in English*. Harvard 1936.

[Simpson, Richard], 'Jane Austen'. *North British Review*, n.s. Vol. xii (1870), pp. 129-52.

Tompkins, J. M. S., *The Popular Novel in England: 1770-1800*. London 1932.

Trilling, Lionel, 'Jane Austen and *Mansfield Park*'. *Partisan Review*, Vol. xxi (1954), pp. 492-511; reprinted in his *The Opposing Self*. New York 1955, pp. 206-30.

——, Introduction to *Emma*. Boston 1957. Reprinted as '*Emma* and the Legend of Jane Austen' in his *Beyond Culture: Essays on Literature and Learning*. London 1966, pp. 31-55.

Watt, Ian, *The Rise of the Novel: Studies in Defoe, Richardson, and Fielding*. London 1957.

——, Introduction to *Jane Austen: A Collection of Critical Essays*. Englewood Cliffs, N.J. 1963, pp. 1-14.

[Whately, Richard], 'Modern Novels'. *Quarterly Review*, Vol. xxiv (1821), pp. 352-76.

Willey, Basil, *The Eighteenth-Century Background: Studies on the Idea of Nature in the Thought of the Period*. London 1940.

Wilson, Edmund, 'A Long Talk about Jane Austen' in Ian Watt (ed.), *Jane Austen*, q.v., pp. 35-40.

Woolf, Virginia, 'Jane Austen' in her *The Common Reader*. London 1925, pp. 191-206.

Wright, Andrew H., *Jane Austen's Novels: A Study in Structure*. London 1953.